GO the DELIVERER

Our Search for Identity and Our Hope for Renewal

STUDY GUIDE | EIGHT SESSIONS

RANDY FRAZEE

Harper*Christian* Resources

God the Deliverer Study Guide
Copyright © 2021 by Randy Frazee

Requests for information should be addressed to: Harper*Christian* Resources,
3900 Sparks Dr. SE, Grand Rapids, Michigan 49546

Content in this study guide is adapted from *The Story Study Guide, The Heart of the Story,*
and *Exploring the Story.*

ISBN 978-0-310-13478-7 (softcover)
ISBN 978-0-310-13479-4 (ebook)

First printing May 2021 / Printed in the United States of America

CONTENTS

HOW TO USE THIS GUIDE

SCOPE AND SEQUENCE

The story of the Bible reveals that heaven and earth are woven more closely together than we might think. All through the Bible, we find two parallel and beautiful dramas unfolding.

There is the **lower story**. Humans live on earth and see things from a horizontal perspective. We can't see what is around the bend but must make decisions on which way to go, where we will live, and how we will respond to what happens to us. We focus on getting through the day as best we can. We interpret why we think other people do what they do. We struggle to know why certain things happen and why other things don't happen.

Then there is the **upper story**. This is how the story is unfolding from God's perspective. Heaven is breaking into our world, and the story of God's seeking love, perpetual grace, and longing for a relationship with ordinary people is breathtaking. Of course, as humans living on this earth, we won't always be able see what is taking place in this upper story. But we can be sure that God is always present, at work, and active in every detail of our lives.

The objective of *God the Deliverer*—the second in a series of three small-group studies in *The Story* series—is to introduce you to these lower and upper stories. In this study, you will examine the disastrous reign of King Saul and the successful reign of King David . . . a former shepherd boy who was a man after God's own heart. You will see how the kingdom broke into two—Israel and Judah—after the reign of King Solomon and how the people of both kingdoms ultimately fell into idolatry. You will witness the consequences when those two kingdoms fall—but also how God always had a plan to deliver his people from their exile.

God wants to be with you. He wants to fill your life with greater purpose, meaning, and understanding. He wants to weave your lower story into his greater upper story that he has been writing. He wants to walk with you in every situation of life. As you recognize how closely his story and your story fit together, you *will* experience his love, grace, and wisdom.

SESSION OUTLINE

Each session is divided into two parts. In the group section, you will watch a video teaching from Randy Frazee and follow along with the outline that has been provided. (Note that you can watch these videos via streaming access at any time by following the instructions found on the inside front cover of this guide.) You will then recite the key verse(s), the key idea, and engage in some guided group discussion through the questions provided. You will close your group with a brief time of prayer.

PERSONAL STUDY

At the end of the group section, you will find a series of readings and study questions for you to go through on your own during the week. The first section will help you *know the story* by asking you to read several key passages from the Bible that were covered during your group time. The next section will help you *understand the story* through a short reading from Randy Frazee that will help you grasp the main takeaways. The third section will help you *live the story* by challenging you to put what you have learned into practice. The final section will help you *tell the story* through a short prompt for a conversation starter around a meal or dinner table. **The personal study is a critical component in helping you grasp the overall story of the Bible, so be sure to complete this study during the week before your next group meeting.**

GROUP SIZE

God the Deliverer can be experienced in a group setting (such as a Bible study, Sunday school class, or small-group gathering) and also as an individual study. If you are doing the study as a group with a large number of participants, it is recommended that everyone watches the video together and then breaks up into smaller groups of four to six for the discussion time. In either case, you can access the teaching videos via the streaming code found on the inside front cover.

MATERIALS NEEDED

Each participant in the group should have his or her own study guide. Although the course can be fully experienced with just the video and study guide, participants are also encouraged to have a copy of *The Story*, which includes selections from the *New International Version* that relate to each week's session.

Reading *The Story* as you go through the study will provide even deeper insights and make the journey even richer and more meaningful.

FACILITATION

Each group should appoint a facilitator who is responsible for keeping track of time during discussions and activities. Facilitators may also read questions aloud and monitor discussions, prompting participants to respond and ensuring everyone that has the opportunity to participate. (For more thorough instructions, refer to the the leader's guide that is included at the back of this guide.)

TIMELINE OF *THE STORY*

TIMELINE OF *GOD THE CREATOR*

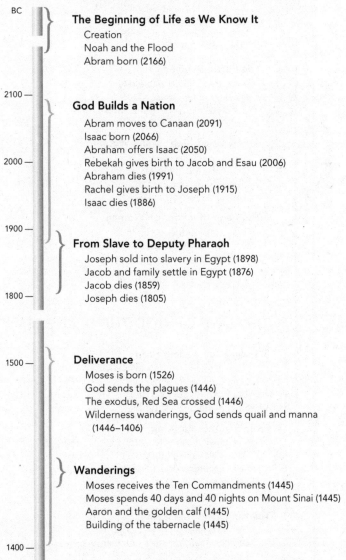

BC

The Beginning of Life as We Know It
Creation
Noah and the Flood
Abram born (2166)

2100 —

God Builds a Nation
Abram moves to Canaan (2091)
Isaac born (2066)
Abraham offers Isaac (2050)
2000 — Rebekah gives birth to Jacob and Esau (2006)
Abraham dies (1991)
Rachel gives birth to Joseph (1915)
Isaac dies (1886)

1900 —

From Slave to Deputy Pharaoh
Joseph sold into slavery in Egypt (1898)
Jacob and family settle in Egypt (1876)
Jacob dies (1859)
1800 — Joseph dies (1805)

Deliverance
1500 — Moses is born (1526)
God sends the plagues (1446)
The exodus, Red Sea crossed (1446)
Wilderness wanderings, God sends quail and manna
(1446–1406)

Wanderings
Moses receives the Ten Commandments (1445)
Moses spends 40 days and 40 nights on Mount Sinai (1445)
Aaron and the golden calf (1445)
Building of the tabernacle (1445)

1400 —

Note: Dates are approximate and dependent on the interpretative theories of various scholars.

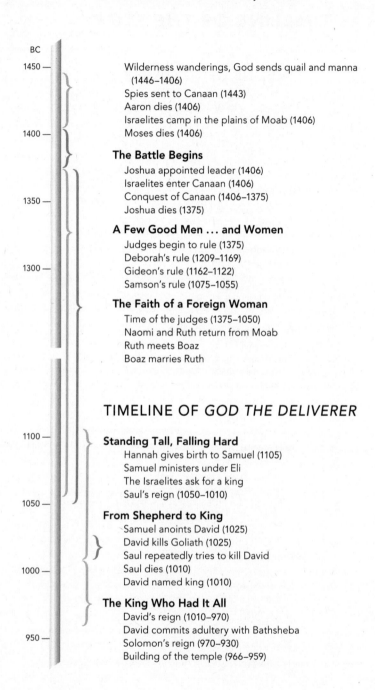

BC

1450 —

Wilderness wanderings, God sends quail and manna
(1446–1406)
Spies sent to Canaan (1443)
Aaron dies (1406)
Israelites camp in the plains of Moab (1406)

1400 —

Moses dies (1406)

The Battle Begins
Joshua appointed leader (1406)
Israelites enter Canaan (1406)
Conquest of Canaan (1406–1375)

1350 —

Joshua dies (1375)

A Few Good Men ... and Women
Judges begin to rule (1375)
Deborah's rule (1209–1169)

1300 —

Gideon's rule (1162–1122)
Samson's rule (1075–1055)

The Faith of a Foreign Woman
Time of the judges (1375–1050)
Naomi and Ruth return from Moab
Ruth meets Boaz
Boaz marries Ruth

TIMELINE OF *GOD THE DELIVERER*

1100 —

Standing Tall, Falling Hard
Hannah gives birth to Samuel (1105)
Samuel ministers under Eli
The Israelites ask for a king
Saul's reign (1050–1010)

1050 —

From Shepherd to King
Samuel anoints David (1025)
David kills Goliath (1025)
Saul repeatedly tries to kill David

1000 —

Saul dies (1010)
David named king (1010)

The King Who Had It All
David's reign (1010–970)
David commits adultery with Bathsheba

950 —

Solomon's reign (970–930)
Building of the temple (966–959)

Timeline of The Story

BC
1000—

David dies (970)
Solomon's reign (970–930)
Solomon displays great wisdom
950—
Building of the temple (966–959)
Solomon marries foreign wives and betrays God

900—

A Kingdom Torn in Two
Division of the kingdom (930)
King Jeroboam I of Israel reigns (930–909)
King Rehoboam of Judah reigns (930–913)
850—
King Ahab of Israel reigns (874–853)
King Jehoshaphat of Judah (872–848)

Elijah's ministry in Israel (875–848)
Elisha's ministry in Israel (c. 848–797)
800—
Amos's ministry in Israel (760–750)
Hosea's ministry in Israel (750–715)

750—

The Kingdoms Fall
Fall of Israel (722)
700—
Exile of Israel to Assyria (722)
Isaiah's ministry in Judah (740–681)
Hezekiah's reign (715–686)

Manasseh's reign (697–642)
650—
Amon's reign (642–640)
Josiah's reign (640–609)
Jeremiah's ministry in Judah (626–585)
Jehoiakim's reign (609–598)
Zedekiah's reign (597–586)
600—
Ezekiel's ministry (593–571)
Fall of Jerusalem (586)

A Prophet in Exile
550—
Daniel exiled to Babylon (605)
Daniel's ministry (605–536)
Nebuchadnezzar's reign (605–562)
Daniel and the lions' den (539)
500—
Fall of Babylon (539)

BC
550—

The Return Home
First return of exiles to Jerusalem (538)
Ministries of Haggai and Zechariah (520–480)
Exiles face opposition in building the temple
Temple restoration completed (516)

500—

The Queen of Beauty and Courage
Xerxes' reign in Persia (486–465)
Esther becomes queen of Persia (479)

450—
Esther saves the Jews from Haman's murderous plot
Days of Purim are established

Second return of exiles to Jerusalem under Ezra (458)
Last group of exiles return to Jerusalem under Nehemiah (445)
400—
Exiles face opposition in rebuilding the wall
Jerusalem's wall rebuilt (445)
Malachi's ministry (c. 440–430)

10—

TIMELINE OF *GOD THE SAVIOR*

5 BC—

Jesus' Birth and Ministry
Mary gives birth to Jesus the Messiah (6/5)
Joseph, Mary, and Jesus' flight to Egypt (5/4)
5 AD—
Jesus' visit to the temple (AD 7/8)

10—

15—

John the Baptist begins ministry (26)
Jesus baptized (26)
20—
Jesus begins ministry (26)
Jesus uses parables to teach (26)
Wedding at Cana (27)
The woman at the well (27)
John the Baptist imprisoned (27/28)
25—
Jesus gives Sermon on the Mount (28)
Jesus sends closest followers out to preach (28)
John the Baptist dies (28/29)
30—
Jesus feeds 5,000 people (29)
Jesus proclaims himself as the bread of life (29)

Timeline of The Story

AD

Jesus, the Son of God
25 —
Jesus teaches at the Mount of Olives (29)
Jesus resurrects Lazarus (29)
Jesus drives the money changers from the temple (30)
Judas betrays Jesus (30)

30 —

The Hour of Darkness
The Lord's Supper (30)
Jesus washes his disciples' feet
35 —
Jesus comforts his disciples
Jesus is arrested
Peter denies Jesus
Jesus is crucified

40 —
The Resurrection
Jesus is buried (30)
Jesus is resurrected
Jesus appears to Mary Magdalene and the disciples

45 —

New Beginnings
Jesus' ascension (30)
50 —
Coming of the Holy Spirit at Pentecost
Paul believed in Jesus as the promised Messiah (35)
James martyred, Peter imprisoned (44)
Paul's first missionary journey (46–48)

55 —
Paul's Mission
Paul's first missionary journey (46–48)
Jerusalem Council (49–50)
Paul's second missionary journey (50–52)
60 —
Paul's third missionary journey (53–57)

Paul's Final Days
Paul's first imprisonment in Rome (59–62)
65 —
Paul's second imprisonment in Rome and execution (67–68)
John exiled on Patmos (90–95)

70 —

The End of Time
John becomes a disciple (26)
John exiled on Patmos (90–95)
Revelation written (95)

90 —

95 —

STANDING TALL, FALLING HARD

1 SAMUEL 1–15

WELCOME

There is a natural desire within each of us to want fit in and be like everyone else. It is in our relational DNA. Just consider the ways we admire people in our society, whether it is a sports star, a talented musician, or an influential leader. We see that person's success and decide we want that in our lives. We want to *be* just like that person we have placed on a pedestal. The people of Israel were no different from us. God had called them as a nation to be different and set apart for him . . . but they wanted to be just like the other nations around them. In particular, they wanted to have a *king.* God had previously warned them of the consequences of having a king—and would warn them again through the prophet Samuel. He always prefers that in our lower story we do things his way. But ultimately, he decided to grant their wish.

—— VIDEO TEACHING NOTES ——

Welcome to session one of *God the Deliverer*. If this is your first time together as a group, take a moment to introduce yourselves. Watch the video (see the streaming video access provided on the inside front cover) and use the following outline to record some of the main points. The answer key is found at the end of the session.

- God is going to reveal his plan through a nation that he has built called _____. God wanted to be their only _____, but they had a different idea in mind.

- God opens the womb of a woman and provides her with a _____. She appropriately names him "_____," which means "heard from God."

- God allows the Israelites to have a human king. It isn't the way that he _____ it unfolding in the lower story, but it doesn't change the ultimate _____ in the upper story. God is still working out his promise to reveal his presence, his power, and his plan to get all people back.

- Samuel tells the Israelites that what they are doing is _____, but that God is allowing it. The warning to both the Israelites and the new king is that they must _____ God. If they don't, it's going to be trouble.

- Saul is _____ God, causing people to get the wrong picture of him—as cruel and greedy versus just and holy.

- God calls Christians to live distinctively different _____. We are challenged by Jesus that although we live in the world, we should not be of the world.

GETTING STARTED

Begin your discussion by reciting the following key verse and key idea together as a group. Now try to state the key verse from memory. On your first attempt, use your notes if you need help. On your second attempt, try to state it completely from memory.

Key Verse: "Does the Lord delight in burnt offerings and sacrifices as much as in obeying the Lord? To obey is better than sacrifice, and to heed is better than the fat of rams" (1 Samuel 15:22).

Key Idea: God wanted to be Israel's only king, but the people wanted a human king so they could be like the surrounding nations. God allows them to select a man named Saul as their king and places his Spirit inside him to empower him. But Saul quickly fails in his mission to represent God and creates consequences in the life of Israel. So God intervenes and removes Saul from the throne.

GROUP DISCUSSION

Take a few minutes with your group members to discuss what you just watched and explore these concepts in Scripture.

1. What part of this week's teaching encouraged or challenged you the most? Why?

2. Why did God want the people of Israel to see *him* as their king?

3. Why did Saul seem like the perfect choice for a human king over Israel?

4. What situation caused God to ultimately reject Saul as king over Israel?

_____

_____

_____

_____

5. How does God call us to live differently today from the rest of the world?

_____

_____

_____

6. What is your biggest takeaway as you reflect on what you learned this week?

_____

_____

_____

_____

CLOSING PRAYER

One of the most important things we can do together in community is to pray for each other. This is not simply a closing prayer to end your group time but a portion of time to share prayer requests and life, to review how God has answered past prayers, and to actually pray for one another. Use the space below to record prayer requests and praises. Also, make sure to pray by name for people God might add to your group—especially your neighbors.

Name   Request/Praise

_____   _____

_____   _____

_____   _____

_____   _____

_____   _____

FOR NEXT WEEK

Next week, we will look at the story of how God raises up a seemingly unimportant shepherd to replace Saul as king over Israel. Before your next group meeting, be sure to read through the following personal study, complete the exercises, and memorize the key verse for the session.

VIDEO NOTES ANSWER KEY

Israel, king / child, Samuel / envisioned, outcome /
wrong, follow / misrepresenting / lifestyles

PERSONAL STUDY

Every session in this guide contains a personal study to help you make meaningful connections between your life and what you are learning each week. Take some time after your group meeting each week to read through this section and complete the personal study. In total, it should take about one hour to complete. Some people like to spread it out, devoting about ten to fifteen minutes a day. Others choose one larger block of time during the week to work through it in one sitting. There is no right or wrong way to do this! Just choose a plan that best fits your needs and schedule and then allow the Scripture to take root in your heart.

KNOW THE STORY

God wanted to be Israel's only king, but the people wanted a human king just like the nations around them. So God determined to honor the people's request for a human king in the lower story without altering his ultimate upper-story objective. If the new king followed the plan of God, things would go well. But if he misrepresented God's name, the Lord would intervene.

> So all the elders of Israel gathered together and came to Samuel at Ramah. They said to him, "You are old, and your sons

do not follow your ways; now appoint a king to lead us, such as all the other nations have."

But when they said, "Give us a king to lead us," this displeased Samuel; so he prayed to the LORD. And the LORD told him: "Listen to all that the people are saying to you; it is not you they have rejected, but they have rejected me as their king. As they have done from the day I brought them up out of Egypt until this day, forsaking me and serving other gods, so they are doing to you. Now listen to them; but warn them solemnly and let them know what the king who will reign over them will claim as his rights." . . .

But the people refused to listen to Samuel. "No!" they said. "We want a king over us. Then we will be like all the other nations, with a king to lead us and to go out before us and fight our battles."

When Samuel heard all that the people said, he repeated it before the LORD. The LORD answered, "Listen to them and give them a king" (1 Samuel 8:4–9, 19–22).

Samuel summoned the people of Israel to the LORD at Mizpah and said to them, "This is what the LORD, the God of Israel, says: 'I brought Israel up out of Egypt, and I delivered you from the power of Egypt and all the kingdoms that oppressed you.' But you have now rejected your God, who saves you out of all your disasters and calamities. And you have said, 'No, appoint a king over us.' So now present yourselves before the LORD by your tribes and clans."

When Samuel had all Israel come forward by tribes, the tribe of Benjamin was taken by lot. Then he brought forward the tribe of Benjamin, clan by clan, and Matri's clan was taken. Finally Saul son of Kish was taken. But when they looked for him, he was not to be found. So they inquired further of the LORD, *"Has the man come here yet?"*

And the LORD *said, "Yes, he has hidden himself among the supplies."*

They ran and brought him out, and as he stood among the people he was a head taller than any of the others. Samuel said to all the people, "Do you see the man the LORD *has chosen? There is no one like him among all the people."*

Then the people shouted, "Long live the king!"

Samuel explained to the people the rights and duties of kingship. He wrote them down on a scroll and deposited it before the LORD. *Then Samuel dismissed the people to go to their own homes* (1 Samuel 10:17–25).

The Philistines assembled to fight Israel, with three thousand chariots, six thousand charioteers, and soldiers as numerous as the sand on the seashore. They went up and camped at Mikmash, east of Beth Aven. When the Israelites saw that their situation was critical and that their army was hard pressed, they hid in caves and thickets, among the rocks, and in pits and cisterns. Some Hebrews even crossed the Jordan to the land of Gad and Gilead.

Saul remained at Gilgal, and all the troops with him were quaking with fear. He waited seven days, the time set by Samuel; but Samuel did not come to Gilgal, and Saul's men began to scatter. So he said, "Bring me the burnt offering and the fellowship offerings." And Saul offered up the burnt offering. Just as he finished making the offering, Samuel arrived, and Saul went out to greet him.

"What have you done?" asked Samuel.

Saul replied, "When I saw that the men were scattering, and that you did not come at the set time, and that the Philistines were assembling at Mikmash, I thought, 'Now the Philistines will come down against me at Gilgal, and I have not sought the LORD's favor.' So I felt compelled to offer the burnt offering."

"You have done a foolish thing," Samuel said. "You have not kept the command the LORD your God gave you; if you had, he would have established your kingdom over Israel for all time. But now your kingdom will not endure; the LORD has sought out a man after his own heart and appointed him ruler of his people, because you have not kept the LORD's command" (1 Samuel 13:5–14).

Then Saul attacked the Amalekites all the way from Havilah to Shur, near the eastern border of Egypt. He took Agag king of the Amalekites alive, and all his people he totally destroyed with the sword. But Saul and the army spared Agag and the best of the sheep and cattle, the fat calves and lambs—everything that was good. These they were unwilling to destroy completely, but everything that was despised and weak they totally destroyed.

Then the word of the LORD came to Samuel: "I regret that I have made Saul king, because he has turned away from me and has not carried out my instructions." Samuel was angry, and he cried out to the LORD all that night.

Early in the morning Samuel got up and went to meet Saul, but he was told, "Saul has gone to Carmel. There he has set up a monument in his own honor and has turned and gone on down to Gilgal."

When Samuel reached him, Saul said, "The LORD bless you! I have carried out the LORD's instructions."

But Samuel said, "What then is this bleating of sheep in my ears? What is this lowing of cattle that I hear?"

Saul answered, "The soldiers brought them from the Amalekites; they spared the best of the sheep and cattle to sacrifice to the LORD your God, but we totally destroyed the rest."

"Enough!" Samuel said to Saul. "Let me tell you what the LORD said to me last night."

"Tell me," Saul replied.

Samuel said, "Although you were once small in your own eyes, did you not become the head of the tribes of Israel? The LORD anointed you king over Israel. And he sent you on a mission, saying, 'Go and completely destroy those wicked people, the Amalekites; wage war against them until you have wiped them out.' Why did you not obey the LORD? Why did you pounce on the plunder and do evil in the eyes of the LORD?"

"But I did obey the LORD," Saul said. "I went on the mission the LORD assigned me. I completely destroyed the Amalekites and brought back Agag their king. The soldiers took sheep and cattle from the plunder, the best of what was devoted to God, in order to sacrifice them to the LORD your God at Gilgal."

But Samuel replied: "Does the LORD delight in burnt offerings and sacrifices as much as in obeying the LORD? To obey is better than sacrifice, and to heed is better than the fat of rams. For rebellion is like the sin of divination, and arrogance like the evil of idolatry. Because you have rejected the word of the LORD, he has rejected you as king" (1 Samuel 15:7–23).

1. How did God to respond to Samuel when the people asked for a king?

2. How did Saul react when he was chosen by lot to be king?

3. How did Saul disobey the Lord after his victory over the Philistines?

4. How did Saul disobey the Lord after his victory over the Amalekites?

5. How did Samuel respond when Saul claimed that he *had* obeyed the Lord?

_____

_____

_____

_____

_____

UNDERSTAND THE STORY

As a small child, Samuel responded to God's call with a humble invitation: "Speak LORD, for your servant is listening" (1 Samuel 3:9–10). This simple response to God's voice is one of the touchstone moments in Scripture. It models the proper response to the call of God . . . a response marked by a teachable willingness to obey the direction and guidance of the Lord.

Unfortunately, the people of Israel generally failed to make this same kind of response to God. Again and again in their history, we find that *listening to God* is the last thing on their minds and *obeying his word* the last thing in their hearts. Just as they were trapped by their lust for idolatry into the worship of other gods, they have now grown envious of the political might and power of the surrounding nations. All the other countries of the world have kings, but they only have priests and prophets leading them. Kings wore regal robes and jeweled crowns. Priestly garments were quite simple and drab in comparison. Kings could make decisions on the spot. Religious leaders checked in with God first and conferred among themselves.

So, the Israelites demand to have a human monarch of their own. Samuel warns they will ultimately become slaves to this king whom they so desperately desire. But the people persist, so God grants their request. At first, the Israelite experiment in kingship seems to go well. Saul seems to listen to the voice of God. But it doesn't take long for things to change. Saul won all of his early battles, but it was his failure to fully destroy the Amalekites that led to his ultimate rejection as king. So much for godly leadership for God's people!

1. What do the stories you have read this week reveal about willingly obeying God?

_____

_____

_____

_____

2. How do these stories help you understand the importance of listening to God?

_____

_____

_____

_____

LIVE THE STORY

God calls his people to reflect his *character* to the world. When Saul disobeyed the Lord, his actions misrepresented that divine character. As the new king of God's chosen nation, Saul caused people to get the wrong idea of what God was really like. By plundering the possessions of the Amalekites, he became like all the other kings. Just as Saul and the Israelites were God's representatives, so we—as New Testament people—are the representatives of God today. We are the very "body of Christ." In truth, most of the people in our world will get their take on God from *us*. We may be the only Bible they ever read. By living splendidly unlike everyone else, we give them a glimpse into what life in God's community is like. God doesn't want us to be just like everyone else. He wants us to be known by our love. He wants us to look like Jesus.

1. What are the benefits of being different from the world? What are the challenges?

   _____

   _____

   _____

   _____

   _____

   _____

2. What is one action you will take this week to put what you've learned into practice?

   _____

   _____

   _____

   _____

   _____

TELL THE STORY

The goal of this study is not only for you to understand the story of the Bible but also for you to share it with others. So, one day this week around a meal or your dinner table, have an intentional conversation about the topic of this session with family or friends. During your time together, read 1 Samuel 2:1–11, and then use the following question for discussion:

What are some ways you have seen God demonstrate that he is in control?

Ask God this week to help you fully embrace the story of King Saul. Also, spend a few minutes each day committing the key verse to memory: "Does the LORD delight in burnt offerings and sacrifices as much as in obeying the LORD? To obey is better than sacrifice, and to heed is better than the fat of rams" (1 Samuel 15:22).

FROM SHEPHERD TO KING

1 SAMUEL 16–2 SAMUEL 24

WELCOME

In the game of poker, the skill comes in how well players can bluff their opponents. There is one move in particular where players say "all in" and shove their chips to the center of the table. This forces their opponents to either call their bluff (by matching the bet) or fold their hand. In poker, going all in is a huge risk. But with God, it is a sure bet. It's the transaction God proposes that is rewarded with life itself. In the Story, we see that Saul refused to go all in with God . . . and it cost him his throne. But when God looked into the heart of the man we will study this week, he saw an "all in" kind of guy.

VIDEO TEACHING NOTES

Welcome to session two of *God the Deliverer*. If there are any new members in your group, take a moment to introduce yourselves to each other. Spend a few minutes sharing any insights or questions about last week's personal study. Then watch the video (see the streaming video access provided on the inside front cover) and use the following outline to record some of the main points. The answer key is found at the end of the session.

- Saul didn't align his life and reign to the upper story of God. So God communicated to Samuel that it was time to find another king—one who would represent God's _____ and God's _____.

- Jesse didn't bring David off the field from tending sheep because he couldn't see him as even being a _____ for kingship. The Hebrew word Jesse uses to describe his youngest son is our English word "_____."

- David might have been considered a _____ by his father on the outside, but God examined David's heart on the inside and there beheld a _____.

- God allowed Saul to stay in office and chase David for fourteen years to _____ David up so he could handle the pressures of _____ an entire nation.

- God can use our _____ lives as effectively as he uses our _____ lives in the lower story to work out his upper story. However, we miss out on the rich _____ that comes to those who follow God's will.

- David was a _____ in the lower story. His righteous reign points us to the _____ in the upper story.

GETTING STARTED

Begin your discussion by reciting the following key verse and key idea together as a group. Now try to state the key verse from memory. On your first attempt, use your notes if you need help. On your second attempt, try to state it completely from memory.

Key Verse: "The LORD does not look at the things people look at. People look at the outward appearance, but the LORD looks at the heart" (1 Samuel 16:7).

Key Idea: God rejects Saul as king and sends the prophet Samuel to Bethlehem to anoint a shepherd boy named David—a man after his own heart—as Saul's replacement. David is anointed as king, but he will not be inaugurated as king until fourteen long years have passed of being chased by King Saul like a fugitive. God uses this difficult season to grow David's dependency on him and shape him into the kind of man who can handle the pressures of shepherding a nation.

GROUP DISCUSSION

Take a few minutes with your group members to discuss what you just watched and explore these concepts in Scripture.

1. What part of this week's teaching encouraged or challenged you the most? Why?

2. Why didn't Jessie include David in the lineup of his sons for kingship?

3. How did God demonstrate that he was with David after his anointing?

4. What caused Saul to become jealous of David?

_____
_____
_____
_____
_____

5. What does David's story reveal about the kind of people that God is looking to use?

_____
_____
_____
_____
_____

6. What is your biggest takeaway as you reflect on what you learned this week?

_____
_____
_____
_____
_____

CLOSING PRAYER

End your group time by sharing prayer requests, reviewing how God has answered past prayers, and praying for one

another. Use the space below to record any requests and praises. Also, make sure to pray for people God might add to your group—especially your neighbors.

Name   Request/Praise

_____   _____

_____   _____

_____   _____

_____   _____

_____   _____

_____   _____

FOR NEXT WEEK

Next week, we will look at the story of how God blessed one of David's sons—a youth named Solomon—with wisdom and the most amazing kingdom in Israel's history. Before your next group meeting, be sure to read through the following personal study, complete the exercises, and memorize the key verse for the session.

VIDEO NOTES ANSWER KEY

heart, passion / possibility, runt / runt, giant / grow, shepherding / disobedient, obedient, blessing / messiah, Messiah

PERSONAL STUDY

Take some time after your group meeting this week to read through this section and complete the personal study. In total, it should take about one hour to complete. Allow the Scripture to take root in your heart as you review the story of David becoming king over all Israel.

KNOW THE STORY

In our lower stories, we often look at ourselves as if we're undeserving. We think that God couldn't possibly use *us* because we don't have a seminary degree, or are not dynamic speakers, or haven't been a follower of Christ since childhood. We think of ourselves as insignificant—just like the people of David's day viewed him. But David's story reveals that God doesn't judge a person's worth by the world's standards. The Lord looks at the heart.

> The LORD said to Samuel, "How long will you mourn for Saul, since I have rejected him as king over Israel? Fill your horn with oil and be on your way; I am sending you to Jesse of Bethlehem. I have chosen one of his sons to be king.". . .
> Samuel did what the LORD said. When he arrived at Bethlehem, the elders of the town trembled when they met him. They asked, "Do you come in peace?"

Samuel replied, "Yes, in peace; I have come to sacrifice to the LORD. Consecrate yourselves and come to the sacrifice with me." Then he consecrated Jesse and his sons and invited them to the sacrifice.

When they arrived, Samuel saw Eliab and thought, "Surely the LORD's anointed stands here before the LORD."

But the LORD said to Samuel, "Do not consider his appearance or his height, for I have rejected him. The LORD does not look at the things people look at. People look at the outward appearance, but the LORD looks at the heart."

Then Jesse called Abinadab and had him pass in front of Samuel. But Samuel said, "The LORD has not chosen this one either." Jesse then had Shammah pass by, but Samuel said, "Nor has the LORD chosen this one." Jesse had seven of his sons pass before Samuel, but Samuel said to him, "The LORD has not chosen these." So he asked Jesse, "Are these all the sons you have?"

"There is still the youngest," Jesse answered. "He is tending the sheep."

Samuel said, "Send for him; we will not sit down until he arrives."

So he sent for him and had him brought in. He was glowing with health and had a fine appearance and handsome features.

Then the LORD said, "Rise and anoint him; this is the one."

So Samuel took the horn of oil and anointed him in the presence of his brothers, and from that day on the Spirit of the LORD came powerfully upon David (1 Samuel 16:1, 4–13).

David said to Saul, "Let no one lose heart on account of this Philistine; your servant will go and fight him."

Saul replied, "You are not able to go out against this Philistine and fight him; you are only a young man, and he has been a warrior from his youth."

But David said to Saul, "Your servant has been keeping his father's sheep. When a lion or a bear came and carried off a sheep from the flock, I went after it, struck it and rescued the sheep from its mouth. When it turned on me, I seized it by its hair, struck it and killed it. Your servant has killed both the lion and the bear; this uncircumcised Philistine will be like one of them, because he has defied the armies of the living God. The LORD who rescued me from the paw of the lion and the paw of the bear will rescue me from the hand of this Philistine."

Saul said to David, "Go, and the LORD be with you." . . .

David said to the Philistine, "You come against me with sword and spear and javelin, but I come against you in the name of the LORD Almighty, the God of the armies of Israel, whom you have defied. This day the LORD will deliver you into my hands, and I'll strike you down and cut off your head. This very day I will give the carcasses of the Philistine army to the birds and the wild animals, and the whole world will know that there is a God in Israel. All those gathered here will know that it is not by sword or spear that the LORD saves; for the battle is the LORD's, and he will give all of you into our hands."

As the Philistine moved closer to attack him, David ran quickly toward the battle line to meet him. Reaching into his bag and taking out a stone, he slung it and struck the Philistine on the forehead. The stone sank into his forehead, and he fell facedown on the ground (1 Samuel 17:32–37, 45–49).

Whatever mission Saul sent him on, David was so successful that Saul gave him a high rank in the army. This pleased all the troops, and Saul's officers as well.

When the men were returning home after David had killed the Philistine, the women came out from all the towns of Israel to meet King Saul with singing and dancing, with joyful songs and with timbrels and lyres. As they danced, they sang: "Saul has slain his thousands, and David his tens of thousands."

Saul was very angry; this refrain displeased him greatly. "They have credited David with tens of thousands," he thought, "but me with only thousands. What more can he get but the kingdom?" And from that time on Saul kept a close eye on David.

The next day an evil spirit from God came forcefully on Saul. He was prophesying in his house, while David was playing the lyre, as he usually did. Saul had a spear in his hand and he hurled it, saying to himself, "I'll pin David to the wall." But David eluded him twice.

Saul was afraid of David, because the LORD was with David but had departed from Saul. So he sent David away from him and gave him command over a thousand men, and David led the troops in their campaigns. In everything he did he had great success, because the LORD was with him. When Saul saw how successful he was, he was afraid of him. But all Israel and Judah loved David, because he led them in their campaigns (1 Samuel 18:12–16).

David stayed in the wilderness strongholds and in the hills of the Desert of Ziph. Day after day Saul searched for him, but God did not give David into his hands.

While David was at Horesh in the Desert of Ziph, he learned that Saul had come out to take his life. And Saul's son

Jonathan went to David at Horesh and helped him find strength in God. "Don't be afraid," he said. "My father Saul will not lay a hand on you. You will be king over Israel, and I will be second to you. Even my father Saul knows this." The two of them made a covenant before the LORD. Then Jonathan went home, but David remained at Horesh.

The Ziphites went up to Saul at Gibeah and said, "Is not David hiding among us in the strongholds at Horesh, on the hill of Hakilah, south of Jeshimon? Now, Your Majesty, come down whenever it pleases you to do so, and we will be responsible for giving him into your hands."

Saul replied, "The LORD bless you for your concern for me. Go and get more information. Find out where David usually goes and who has seen him there. They tell me he is very crafty. Find out about all the hiding places he uses and come back to me with definite information. Then I will go with you; if he is in the area, I will track him down among all the clans of Judah."

So they set out and went to Ziph ahead of Saul. Now David and his men were in the Desert of Maon, in the Arabah south of Jeshimon. Saul and his men began the search, and when David was told about it, he went down to the rock and stayed in the Desert of Maon. When Saul heard this, he went into the Desert of Maon in pursuit of David.

Saul was going along one side of the mountain, and David and his men were on the other side, hurrying to get away from Saul. As Saul and his forces were closing in on David and his men to capture them, a messenger came to Saul, saying, "Come quickly! The Philistines are raiding the land." Then Saul broke off his pursuit of David and went to meet the Philistines (1 Samuel 23:14–28).

After Saul returned from pursuing the Philistines, he was told, "David is in the Desert of En Gedi." So Saul took three thousand able young men from all Israel and set out to look for David and his men near the Crags of the Wild Goats.

He came to the sheep pens along the way; a cave was there, and Saul went in to relieve himself. David and his men were far back in the cave. The men said, "This is the day the LORD spoke of when he said to you, 'I will give your enemy into your hands for you to deal with as you wish.'" Then David crept up unnoticed and cut off a corner of Saul's robe.

Afterward, David was conscience-stricken for having cut off a corner of his robe. He said to his men, "The LORD forbid that I should do such a thing to my master, the LORD's anointed, or lay my hand on him; for he is the anointed of the LORD." With these words David sharply rebuked his men and did not allow them to attack Saul. And Saul left the cave and went his way (1 Samuel 24:1–7).

1. What was Samuel's initial thought when he saw Jessie's oldest son?

2. How did David express his faith in God before fighting Goliath?

3. Why was Saul concerned with the refrain that David had slain "tens of thousands"?

4. How did God protect David while he was hiding out in the wilderness?

5. Why was David unwilling to kill Saul in the cave?

UNDERSTAND THE STORY

David's willingness to wait on the Lord defined and refined his character. This faithful dependence on the Lord set him apart from Saul. Although David had been anointed for the kingship, he was willing to wait for God's perfect timing and was unwilling to dishonor the Lord by rushing his timing. David accepted waiting for the kingship, or building the temple, or anything else the Lord might have from him, because he knew God would provide the best.

In Saul, we see a man desperately trying to preserve what he knows is already lost. In David, we see a hero who is all the more admirable due to his unwillingness to grab power under the wrong circumstances. David's true heart was revealed in the midst of those struggles. The same trust in the Lord that led him to fight Goliath and the Philistines sustained him as he camped out in caves and hid from his enemies.

David's experiences in the desert taught him that God always keeps his promises. Even when David sinned, he ultimately humbled himself before the Lord, repented, and sought to be obedient to his God. As he wrote, "Have mercy on me, O God, according to your unfailing love; according to your great compassion blot out my transgressions" (Psalm 51:1). David was truly a man after God's heart . . . and a man who was willing to wait on God's timing.

1. What do the stories you have read this week reveal about the heart God wants his people to have?

2. How will these stories help you understand what it means to follow God's plan for you?

LIVE THE STORY

David's story reveals that God is looking for people who love him with all of their heart, soul, mind, and strength (see Mark 12:30). No other qualifications are necessary! In the lower stories, you may see yourself as just a grimy field hand who is only good enough to tend sheep. You don't look in the mirror and see anything that could be considered "king material." But God sees you differently. As Peter wrote, "You are a chosen people, a royal priesthood, a holy nation, God's special possession" (1 Peter 2:9). He has giants for you to kill— audacious plans to accomplish that require someone like David to get the job done. He knows that with your willingness to go all in for him, and *his* power to transform you, nothing is impossible.

1. What does it mean to be "all in" and completely committed to Jesus?

2. What is one action you will take this week to put what you've learned into practice?

TELL THE STORY

One day this week around a meal or your dinner table, have an intentional conversation about the topic of this session with family or friends. During your time together, read 1 Samuel 17:20–50, and then use the following question for discussion:

> *How did David see the battle against Goliath as compared to the other Israelites?*

Ask God this week to help you fully embrace the story of David. Also, spend a few minutes each day committing the key verse to memory: "The LORD does not look at the things people look at. People look at the outward appearance, but the LORD looks at the heart" (1 Samuel 16:7).

THE KING WHO
HAD IT ALL

1 KINGS 1–11

WELCOME

If you could have anything you wanted by just asking for it . . . what would it be? Be honest. If you are like most people, you would likely ask for money. Or the skills and talents that would make you famous enough to earns lots of money. You would then want a luxury automobile, a bazillion-square-foot house, and the ability to take lavish vacations. While many of us would like to think we would do something to help the disadvantaged . . . the temptation would be to ask for wealth to make ourselves more comfortable in this life. This is why Solomon's story is so surprising. Early in his reign, the Lord comes to him and says he can have anything he wants. Solomon asks for *wisdom*. The request is not so much for himself but for his people. He wants the wisdom to be able to lead them. Solomon started so well. But would he *finish* well?

VIDEO TEACHING NOTES

Welcome to session three of *God the Deliverer*. Spend a few minutes sharing any insights or questions about last week's personal study. Then watch the video (see the streaming video access provided on the inside front cover). The answer key is found at the end of the session.

- God tells Solomon to ask him for anything he wants. Solomon asks for _wisdom_ to carry out his duties, govern the people, and discern right from wrong. God _answers_ his request and also gives him wealth, honor, and power to boot.

- Solomon wrote his wisdom down. _Proverbs_ , _Ecclesiastes_ , and Song of _Solomon_ are filled with "lukewarm pots of water" we should avoid.

- God tells Solomon that if he continues to follow the Lord, he will finish _strong_ and pass the kingdom to his son in the same great shape that David did for him. But if he doesn't follow the Lord, he will get _cooked_ .

- Solomon jumped into one of the proverbial pots of _lukewarm_ water that he writes about. As time passed the pot began to simmer, and Solomon's strength weakened. He started *worshipping* other gods.

- God has put people into our lives. How we live our lives in Christ before them will give *witness* that Jesus is not dead but alive and *resurrected*. In other words, how we live our lives matters.

- Here is best thing Solomon ever taught us—it's never too *late* to come back to God. And if you do, he will *receive* you with open arms.

GETTING STARTED

Begin your discussion by reciting the following key verse and key idea together as a group. Now try to state the key verse from memory. On your first attempt, use your notes if you need help. On your second attempt, try to state it completely from memory.

Key Verse: "Now all has been heard; here is the conclusion of the matter: Fear God and keep his commandments, for this is the duty of all mankind" (Ecclesiastes 12:13).

Key Idea: Solomon receives the throne from his father, King David, in the best possible condition. In the early years of his reign, the Lord comes to Solomon and grants his request to receive wisdom. Solomon makes wise decisions that are in alignment with God's will, and the nation is blessed beyond measure. But later, Solomon loses his way. He marries foreign women who worship other gods, which ultimately leads him to compromise Israel's witness to other nations.

GROUP DISCUSSION

Take a few minutes with your group members to discuss what you just watched and explore these concepts in Scripture.

1. What part of this week's teaching encouraged or challenged you the most? Why?

2. Why did Solomon desire to have wisdom from God?

3. What are some of the ways that Solomon demonstrated he received this wisdom?

4. What compromises did Solomon begin to make during his reign?

_____

_____

_____

_____

5. How did these compromises ultimately impact his relationship with God?

_____

_____

_____

_____

6. What is your biggest takeaway as you reflect on what you learned this week?

_____

_____

_____

_____

CLOSING PRAYER

End your group time by sharing prayer requests, reviewing how God has answered past prayers, and praying for one another. Use the space below to record any requests and praises.

Also, make sure to pray for people God might add to your group—especially your neighbors.

Name   Request/Praise

_____   _____

_____   _____

_____   _____

_____   _____

_____   _____

_____   _____

——— FOR NEXT WEEK ———

Next week, we will look at the story of how the kingdom of Israel was torn into two after the death of Solomon because of a young king who listened to poor counsel. Before your next group meeting, be sure to read through the following personal study, complete the exercises, and memorize the key verse for the session.

VIDEO NOTES ANSWER KEY

wisdom, answers / Proverbs, Ecclesiastes, Solomon /
strong, cooked / lukewarm, worshiping / witness,
resurrected / late, receive

PERSONAL STUDY

Take some time after your group meeting this week to read through this section and complete the personal study. In total, it should take about one hour to complete. Allow the Scripture to take root in your heart and ask God to help you understand the story of Solomon.

KNOW THE STORY

The wisdom that Solomon received from God enabled him to become a great builder. He built a grand palace and temple to the Lord. He built stables, chariots, and storehouses. He built a bureaucratic system and alliances with other nations. He constructed proverbs, love poems, and works of philosophy. But toward the end of his reign, Solomon also built altars to foreign gods. Even as he was externally building structures and systems that would strengthen his kingdom, internally he was building practices that would destroy it.

The king went to Gibeon to offer sacrifices, for that was the most important high place, and Solomon offered a thousand burnt offerings on that altar. At Gibeon the LORD appeared to Solomon during the night in a dream, and God said, "Ask for whatever you want me to give you."

Solomon answered, "You have shown great kindness to your servant, my father David, because he was faithful to you and righteous and upright in heart. You have continued this great kindness to him and have given him a son to sit on his throne this very day.

"Now, Lord my God, you have made your servant king in place of my father David. But I am only a little child and do not know how to carry out my duties. Your servant is here among the people you have chosen, a great people, too numerous to count or number. So give your servant a discerning heart to govern your people and to distinguish between right and wrong. For who is able to govern this great people of yours?"

The Lord was pleased that Solomon had asked for this. So God said to him, "Since you have asked for this and not for long life or wealth for yourself, nor have asked for the death of your enemies but for discernment in administering justice, I will do what you have asked. I will give you a wise and discerning heart, so that there will never have been anyone like you, nor will there ever be. Moreover, I will give you what you have not asked for—both wealth and honor—so that in your lifetime you will have no equal among kings. And if you walk in obedience to me and keep my decrees and commands as David your father did, I will give you a long life." Then Solomon awoke—and he realized it had been a dream (1 Kings 3:4–15).

Now two prostitutes came to the king and stood before him. One of them said, "Pardon me, my lord. This woman and I live in the same house, and I had a baby while she was there with me. The third day after my child was born, this woman also had a baby. We were alone; there was no one in the house but the two of us.

"During the night this woman's son died because she lay on him. So she got up in the middle of the night and took my son from my side while I your servant was asleep. She put him by her breast and put her dead son by my breast. The next morning, I got up to nurse my son—and he was dead! But when I looked at him closely in the morning light, I saw that it wasn't the son I had borne."

The other woman said, "No! The living one is my son; the dead one is yours."

But the first one insisted, "No! The dead one is yours; the living one is mine." And so they argued before the king.

The king said, "This one says, 'My son is alive and your son is dead,' while that one says, 'No! Your son is dead and mine is alive.'"

Then the king said, "Bring me a sword." So they brought a sword for the king. He then gave an order: "Cut the living child in two and give half to one and half to the other."

The woman whose son was alive was deeply moved out of love for her son and said to the king, "Please, my lord, give her the living baby! Don't kill him!"

But the other said, "Neither I nor you shall have him. Cut him in two!"

Then the king gave his ruling: "Give the living baby to the first woman. Do not kill him; she is his mother."

When all Israel heard the verdict the king had given, they held the king in awe, because they saw that he had wisdom from God to administer justice (1 Kings 3:16–28).

The priests then brought the ark of the LORD's covenant to its place in the inner sanctuary of the temple, the Most Holy Place, and put it beneath the wings of the cherubim. The cherubim spread their wings over the place of the ark and overshadowed the ark and its carrying poles. These poles were so long that their ends could be seen from the Holy Place in front of the inner sanctuary, but not from outside the Holy Place; and they are still there today. There was nothing in the ark except the two stone tablets that Moses had placed in it at Horeb, where the LORD made a covenant with the Israelites after they came out of Egypt.

When the priests withdrew from the Holy Place, the cloud filled the temple of the LORD. And the priests could not perform their service because of the cloud, for the glory of the LORD filled his temple.

Then Solomon said, "The LORD has said that he would dwell in a dark cloud; I have indeed built a magnificent temple for you, a place for you to dwell forever."

While the whole assembly of Israel was standing there, the king turned around and blessed them. Then he said:

"Praise be to the LORD, the God of Israel, who with his own hand has fulfilled what he promised with his own mouth to my father David. For he said, 'Since the day I brought my people Israel out of Egypt, I have not chosen a city in any tribe of Israel to have a temple built so that my Name might be there, but I have chosen David to rule my people Israel.'

"My father David had it in his heart to build a temple for the Name of the LORD, the God of Israel. But the LORD said to my father David, 'You did well to have it in your heart to build a temple for my Name. Nevertheless, you are not the one to build the temple, but your son, your own flesh and blood—he is the one who will build the temple for my Name.'

"The LORD has kept the promise he made: I have succeeded David my father and now I sit on the throne of Israel, *just as the* LORD *promised, and I have built the temple for the Name of the* LORD*, the God of Israel. I have provided a place there for the ark, in which is the covenant of the* LORD *that he made with our ancestors when he brought them out of Egypt"* (1 Kings 8:6–21).

When Solomon had finished building the temple of the LORD *and the royal palace, and had achieved all he had desired to do, the* LORD *appeared to him a second time, as he had appeared to him at Gibeon. The* LORD *said to him:*

"I have heard the prayer and plea you have made before me; I have consecrated this temple, which you have built, by putting my Name there forever. My eyes and my heart will always be there.

"As for you, if you walk before me faithfully with integrity of heart and uprightness, as David your father did, and do all I command and observe my decrees and laws, I will establish your royal throne over Israel forever, as I promised David your father when I said, 'You shall never fail to have a successor on the throne of Israel.'

"But if you or your descendants turn away from me and do not observe the commands and decrees I have given you and go off to serve other gods and worship them, then I will cut off Israel from the land I have given them and will reject this temple I have consecrated for my Name" (1 Kings 9:1–7).

King Solomon, however, loved many foreign women besides Pharaoh's daughter—Moabites, Ammonites, Edomites, Sidonians and Hittites. They were from nations about which the LORD *had told the Israelites, "You must not intermarry*

*with them, because they will surely turn your hearts after
their gods." Nevertheless, Solomon held fast to them in love.
He had seven hundred wives of royal birth and three hundred concubines, and his wives led him astray. As Solomon
grew old, his wives turned his heart after other gods, and his
heart was not fully devoted to the LORD his God, as the heart
of David his father had been*

*On a hill east of Jerusalem, Solomon built a high place
for Chemosh the detestable god of Moab, and for Molek the
detestable god of the Ammonites. He did the same for all his
foreign wives, who burned incense and offered sacrifices to
their gods.*

*The LORD became angry with Solomon because his heart
had turned away from the LORD, the God of Israel, who had
appeared to him twice. Although he had forbidden Solomon
to follow other gods, Solomon did not keep the LORD's command. So the LORD said to Solomon, "Since this is your attitude and you have not kept my covenant and my decrees,
which I commanded you, I will most certainly tear the kingdom away from you and give it to one of your subordinates.
Nevertheless, for the sake of David your father, I will not do
it during your lifetime"* (1 Kings 11:1–12).

1. How did God respond when Solomon asked to receive
   wisdom?

   _____

   _____

   _____

   _____

   _____

2. How did Solomon decide the rightful mother of the child in the case brought to him?

_____

_____

_____

_____

_____

_____

3. What happened when the ark of the covenant was brought into the temple?

_____

_____

_____

_____

_____

_____

4. What did God say to Solomon the second time that he appeared to him?

_____

_____

_____

_____

_____

_____

5. What did Solomon begin to do in violation of God's commands?

_____

_____

_____

_____

_____

_____

_____

UNDERSTAND THE STORY

At the beginning of Solomon's story, we read that he "showed his love for the Lord by walking according to the instructions given him by his father David" (1 Kings 3:3). Solomon's talents, skills, and leadership were exceptional. He made the right choice at the beginning of his reign by asking God for wisdom to lead the people. He walked with the Lord.

However, we also find this caveat at the beginning of Solomon's story: "Except that he offered sacrifices and burned incense on the high places" (verse 3). Ultimately, it was the "except thats" in Solomon's life that came to define him and his reign. Solomon seemed to be the perfect king—a rock star for God and his nation. But in addition to having palaces filled with the most exquisite stuff, Solomon also had 700 wives and 300 concubines .

According to the customs of the day, this wasn't unusual or wrong in God's sight. But Solomon took wives from other nations in disobedience to God's rules. The Lord had warned the Israelites not to marry people from other nations because it could lead to them worshiping foreign gods. Solomon probably thought he was too wise to let his wives turn him away from God. At first, he was right. We don't know if his fall began after twenty years of ruling Israel or thirty years into his reign. But eventually, the water got too hot for him. The Bible tells us is that "as Solomon grew old, his wives turned his heart after other gods" (1 Kings 11:4).

1. What do the stories you have read this week reveal about being faithful to God?

2. How do these stories help you realize the importance of complete obedience to God?

LIVE THE STORY

Solomon's story shows us that falling away from God doesn't happen overnight. Rather, it is composed of a succession of smaller compromises that eventually leads to a total collapse. In our lives, we may think we're stuck with "rules" from God that keep us from having any fun. We might convince ourselves that we can dabble outside of those rules and still maintain our strength to resist. But as the apostle Paul wrote, "So, if you think you are standing firm, be careful that you don't fall!" (1 Corinthians 10:12). How we live our lives *matters*. Our prayer must be that we will not only start strong but also finish strong. And if we succumb to compromise, we must remember that with God it is never too late to come back to him.

1. In what ways have been you tempted to compromise on God's best for you?

   _____

   _____

   _____

2. What is one action you will take this week to put what you've learned into practice?

   _____

   _____

   _____

   _____

TELL THE STORY

One day around a meal or your dinner table, have an intentional conversation about this week's topic with family or friends. During your time together, read Proverbs 16:1–9, which was written by King Solomon, and then use the following question for discussion:

What do these proverbs say about following our plans versus God's plans?

Ask God this week to help you fully embrace the story of Solomon and his failure to resist compromises. Also, spend a few minutes each day committing the key verse to memory: "Now all has been heard; here is the conclusion of the matter: Fear God and keep his commandments, for this is the duty of all mankind" (Ecclesiastes 12:13).

A KINGDOM TORN IN TWO

1 KINGS 12–2 KINGS 16

WELCOME

Military aviators have an interesting saying about a plane crash that is imminent: "The accident has already occurred . . . we are just waiting for the plane to arrive at the crash site." What does this mean? The "accident" occurred miles before the actual crash of the plane, when the pilot or a member of the crew made a fatal decision. Perhaps this accident occurred before the plane ever left the ground due to a manufacturing flaw or due to a maintenance oversight. Now, it is just a matter of waiting until the plane actually crashes. This is precisely what we find happening in this next section of God's Story as King Solomon approaches the end of his reign over Israel.

——— VIDEO TEACHING NOTES ———

Welcome to session four of *God the Deliverer*. Spend a few minutes sharing any insights or questions about last week's personal study. Then watch the video (see the streaming video access provided on the inside front cover). The answer key is found at the end of the session.

- Toward the end of King Solomon's reign, he became aggressive with building projects. To pay for it, he ___overtaxed___ the people and forced them to ___participate___ in hard labor. Solomon dies, and the throne is passed to his son, Rehoboam.

- Jeroboam was a successful and capable officer in Solomon's cabinet who had ___rebelled___ and fled Israel. When King Solomon dies, he feels this might be a good opportunity to come home and appeal to Rehoboam for ___relief___ .

- Rehoboam listens to the advice of the _____ _____ he grew up with and rejects Jeroboam's request. So Jeroboam takes the ten northern tribes and forms a nation called ___young___ . Rehoboam stays on as king to the two remaining tribes in the south—Judah and Benjamin. Their nation is called ___Israel___ ___Judah___ .

- The once mighty nation that God had built from scratch—the talk of the world and unstoppable in all ways—had now been severely ___weakened___ . And not by an outside enemy . . . but from within.

- It appears from the lower story that the cause of this conflict was Rehoboam's _decision_. God certainly used this event, but the ultimate cause was God. This leads to a greater theme: "A house _____ against God cannot stand."

- To experience the full blessings of God—and to ensure that everything works out for the _good_ in our life—we need to be fully devoted to God above all and _align_ our lives to his upper story plan.

GETTING STARTED

Begin your discussion by reciting the following key verse and key idea together as a group. Now try to state the key verse from memory. On your first attempt, use your notes if you need help. On your second attempt, try to state it completely from memory.

Key Verse: "'This is what the LORD says: Do not go up to fight against your brothers, the Israelites. Go home, every one of you, for this is my doing.' So they obeyed the word of the LORD and went home again" (1 Kings 12:24).

Key Idea: King Solomon had overtaxed the people and forced them to labor in his building projects. After his death, Jeroboam comes before the new king, Rehoboam, to plead for these burdens to be lifted. But Rehoboam listens to poor advice and vows to work the people even harder. This leads to the ten tribes in the north becoming the nation of Israel and the two tribes in the south becoming the nation of Judah. In the lower story, the nation of Israel seems to have divided because of the immature response of Rehoboam. But from the upper story point of view, we learn that the division comes as a part of God's greater plan.

GROUP DISCUSSION

Take a few minutes with your group members to discuss what you just watched and explore these concepts in Scripture.

1. What part of this week's teaching encouraged or challenged you the most? Why?

2. What was the setting of the story that led to Jeroboam's complaint?

3. What two sets of advice did Rehoboam receive on how to handle the problem?

_____

_____

_____

_____

_____

4. Why did God ultimately allow this division to take place?

_____

_____

_____

_____

5. What does this story reveal about what happens when we divide our loyalty to God?

_____

_____

_____

_____

_____

6. What is your biggest takeaway as you reflect on what you learned this week?

_____

_____

_____

_____

_____

CLOSING PRAYER

End your group time by sharing prayer requests, reviewing how God has answered past prayers, and praying for one another. Use the space below to record any requests and praises. Also, make sure to pray for people God might add to your group—especially your neighbors.

Name   Request/Praise

_____   _____

_____   _____

_____   _____

_____   _____

_____   _____

FOR NEXT WEEK

Next week, we will look at how the idolatry of God's people led to the downfall of Israel in the north (at the hands of the Assyrians) and then to Judah in the south (at the hands of the Babylonians). Before your next group meeting, be sure to read through the following personal study, complete the exercises, and memorize the key verse for the session.

VIDEO NOTES ANSWER KEY

overtaxed, participate / rebelled, relief / young men, Israel, Judah / weakened / decision, divided / good, align

PERSONAL STUDY

Take some time after your group meeting this week to read through this section and complete the personal study. In total, it should take about one hour to complete. Allow the Scripture to take root in your heart as you review the story of how Israel was divided into two nations.

KNOW THE STORY

When the people of Israel first demanded a king, the prophet Samuel warned, "He will take your sons and make them serve with his chariots and horses" (1 Samuel 8:11). Within three generations, this prophecy concerning the monarchy came true. By the time Rehoboam assumed the throne, the dream for a strong king to unite the nation had become a nightmare. The monarchy would now become one of the key sources of the nation's undoing.

> *Rehoboam went to Shechem, for all Israel had gone there to make him king. When Jeroboam son of Nebat heard this (he was still in Egypt, where he had fled from King Solomon), he returned from Egypt. So they sent for Jeroboam, and he and the whole assembly of Israel went to Rehoboam and said to him: "Your father put a heavy yoke on us, but now lighten the harsh labor and the heavy yoke he put on us, and we will serve you."*

Rehoboam answered, "Go away for three days and then come back to me." So the people went away.

Then King Rehoboam consulted the elders who had served his father Solomon during his lifetime. "How would you advise me to answer these people?" he asked.

They replied, "If today you will be a servant to these people and serve them and give them a favorable answer, they will always be your servants."

But Rehoboam rejected the advice the elders gave him and consulted the young men who had grown up with him and were serving him. He asked them, "What is your advice? How should we answer these people who say to me, 'Lighten the yoke your father put on us'?"

The young men who had grown up with him replied, "These people have said to you, 'Your father put a heavy yoke on us, but make our yoke lighter.' Now tell them, 'My little finger is thicker than my father's waist. My father laid on you a heavy yoke; I will make it even heavier. My father scourged you with whips; I will scourge you with scorpions.'"

Three days later Jeroboam and all the people returned to Rehoboam, as the king had said, "Come back to me in three days." The king answered the people harshly. Rejecting the advice given him by the elders, he followed the advice of the young men and said, "My father made your yoke heavy; I will make it even heavier. My father scourged you with whips; I will scourge you with scorpions." So the king did not listen to the people, for this turn of events was from the LORD, to fulfill the word the LORD had spoken to Jeroboam son of Nebat through Ahijah the Shilonite.

When all Israel saw that the king refused to listen to them, they answered the king: "What share do we have in

David, what part in Jesse's son? To your tents, Israel! Look after your own house, David!"

So the Israelites went home. But as for the Israelites who were living in the towns of Judah, Rehoboam still ruled over them.

King Rehoboam sent out Adoniram, who was in charge of forced labor, but all Israel stoned him to death. King Rehoboam, however, managed to get into his chariot and escape to Jerusalem. So Israel has been in rebellion against the house of David to this day.

When all the Israelites heard that Jeroboam had returned, they sent and called him to the assembly and made him king over all Israel. Only the tribe of Judah remained loyal to the house of David.

When Rehoboam arrived in Jerusalem, he mustered all Judah and the tribe of Benjamin—a hundred and eighty thousand able young men—to go to war against Israel and to regain the kingdom for Rehoboam son of Solomon.

But this word of God came to Shemaiah the man of God: "Say to Rehoboam son of Solomon king of Judah, to all Judah and Benjamin, and to the rest of the people, 'This is what the LORD says: Do not go up to fight against your brothers, the Israelites. Go home, every one of you, for this is my doing.'" So they obeyed the word of the LORD and went home again, as the LORD had ordered (1 Kings 12:1–24).

Then Jeroboam fortified Shechem in the hill country of Ephraim and lived there. From there he went out and built up Peniel.

Jeroboam thought to himself, "The kingdom will now likely revert to the house of David. If these people go up to offer sacrifices at the temple of the LORD *in Jerusalem, they will again give their allegiance to their lord, Rehoboam king of Judah. They will kill me and return to King Rehoboam."*

After seeking advice, the king made two golden calves. He said to the people, "It is too much for you to go up to Jerusalem. Here are your gods, Israel, who brought you up out of Egypt." One he set up in Bethel, and the other in Dan. And this thing became a sin; the people came to worship the one at Bethel and went as far as Dan to worship the other.

Jeroboam built shrines on high places and appointed priests from all sorts of people, even though they were not Levites. He instituted a festival on the fifteenth day of the eighth month, like the festival held in Judah, and offered sacrifices on the altar. This he did in Bethel, sacrificing to the calves he had made. And at Bethel he also installed priests at the high places he had made. On the fifteenth day of the eighth month, a month of his own choosing, he offered sacrifices on the altar he had built at Bethel. So he instituted the festival for the Israelites and went up to the altar to make offerings (1 Kings 12:25–33).

At that time Abijah son of Jeroboam became ill, and Jeroboam said to his wife, "Go, disguise yourself, so you won't be recognized as the wife of Jeroboam. Then go to Shiloh. Ahijah the prophet is there—the one who told me I would be king over this people. Take ten loaves of bread with you, some cakes and a jar of honey, and go to him. He will tell you what will happen to the boy." So Jeroboam's wife did what he said and went to Ahijah's house in Shiloh.

Now Ahijah could not see; his sight was gone because of his age. But the LORD *had told Ahijah, "Jeroboam's wife is coming to ask you about her son, for he is ill, and you are to give her such and such an answer. When she arrives, she will pretend to be someone else."*

So when Ahijah heard the sound of her footsteps at the door, he said, "Come in, wife of Jeroboam. Why this pretense? I have been sent to you with bad news. Go, tell Jeroboam that this is what the LORD, the God of Israel, says: 'I raised you up from among the people and appointed you ruler over my people Israel. I tore the kingdom away from the house of David and gave it to you, but you have not been like my servant David, who kept my commands and followed me with all his heart, doing only what was right in my eyes. You have done more evil than all who lived before you. You have made for yourself other gods, idols made of metal; you have aroused my anger and turned your back on me.

"'Because of this, I am going to bring disaster on the house of Jeroboam. I will cut off from Jeroboam every last male in Israel—slave or free. I will burn up the house of Jeroboam as one burns dung, until it is all gone. Dogs will eat those belonging to Jeroboam who die in the city, and the birds will feed on those who die in the country. The LORD has spoken!'" (1 Kings 14:1–11).

Rehoboam son of Solomon was king in Judah. He was forty-one years old when he became king, and he reigned seventeen years in Jerusalem, the city the LORD had chosen out of all the tribes of Israel in which to put his Name. His mother's name was Naamah; she was an Ammonite.

Judah did evil in the eyes of the LORD. By the sins they committed they stirred up his jealous anger more than those who were before them had done. They also set up for themselves high places, sacred stones and Asherah poles on every high hill and under every spreading tree. There were even male shrine prostitutes in the land; the people engaged in all the detestable practices of the nations the LORD had driven out before the Israelites.

In the fifth year of King Rehoboam, Shishak king of Egypt attacked Jerusalem. He carried off the treasures of the temple of the LORD and the treasures of the royal palace. He took everything, including all the gold shields Solomon had made. So King Rehoboam made bronze shields to replace them and assigned these to the commanders of the guard on duty at the entrance to the royal palace. Whenever the king went to the LORD's temple, the guards bore the shields, and afterward they returned them to the guardroom (1 Kings 14:21–28).

1. How did Rehoboam choose to respond to the people's complaints?

2. What caused Rehoboam to cease his attack against the rebelling tribes?

3. What caused Jeroboam to set up false gods for his people to worship?

_____

_____

_____

4. What did the prophet Ahijah say would happen as a result of Jeroboam's sin?

_____

_____

_____

_____

5. How did Rehoboam likewise fail in his leadership of Judah and Benjamin?

_____

_____

_____

_____

UNDERSTAND THE STORY

God wanted to use the nation of Israel to reveal his character to the rest of the world so that all people would want to do life with him. When the Israelites got along, foreign nations caught a glimpse of what it would be like to be part of God's family, and the Lord prospered them. When they turned their backs on God, they no longer accurately reflected his character and the kind of community he wanted to build, so the Lord had to discipline them.

From a lower story point of view, Israel was divided because of the immature response of Rehoboam. But from the upper story point of view, the division came about due to God's plan. As Rehoboam readied his forces to launch an attack against the northern rebel kingdom, God stepped in and said, "This is my doing" (1 Kings 12:24). It was as if he were saying, "I knew you would heed the advice of your yes-men. I knew Jeroboam would rebel against you. And I knew you would do everything in your power to bring your divided kingdom back together. But it's in my power, not yours. So go home. Your role in this movie is just about over."

This discipline from God had come about as a direct result of the people's disobedience and worship of foreign gods. As the author of Hebrews would later put it: "What children are not disciplined by their father? If you are not disciplined—and everyone undergoes discipline—then you are not legitimate, not true sons and daughters at all. . . . No discipline seems pleasant at the time, but painful. Later on, however, it produces a harvest of righteousness and peace for those who have been trained by it" (Hebrews 12:7–8, 11).

1. What do these stories you have read this week reveal about God's discipline?

_____

_____

_____

_____

_____

2. How will these stories help you respond when you encounter God's discipline?

_____

_____

_____

_____

LIVE THE STORY

The story of Rehoboam and Jeroboam is tragic because both men ultimately turned their backs on God. In the process, they did great damage both to the way their people viewed the Lord and how the other nations viewed him. In the same way, nothing harms the church today more than when its people reflect the wrong image of God. We do this whenever we treat others unkindly or unfairly—especially the poor, the widows, and the strangers in our midst. We do this whenever we conduct our business dishonestly or let our anger get the best of us. We do this whenever we withhold our love from others and refuse to serve them in humility. God gives us a _privilege_ and a _responsibility_ to show others what he is truly like. The way we live has consequences—for it can either give others a negative picture of God or a positive one.

1. What image of God are others seeing by the way you lead your life?

_____

_____

_____

2. What is one action you will take this week to put what you've learned into practice?

_____

_____

_____

_____

_____

TELL THE STORY

One day around a meal or your dinner table, have an intentional conversation about this week's topic with family or friends. During your time together, read 1 Kings 12:1–11, and then use the following question for discussion:

What pieces of advice have you received and put into practice?

Ask God this week to help you fully embrace the warnings in the stories of Rehoboam and Jeroboam. Also, spend a few minutes each day committing the key verse to memory: "'This is what the LORD says: Do not go up to fight against your brothers, the Israelites. Go home, every one of you, for this is my doing.' So they obeyed the word of the LORD and went home again" (1 Kings 12:24).

THE KINGDOMS FALL

2 KINGS 17–25

WELCOME

As you look at the stories of Israel and Judah, two nations whose kings got them into a heap of trouble, you have to wonder whether holding to a motto like "no king but God" would have led to different outcomes. Throughout 208 years under 39 kings, both kingdoms repeatedly turned their backs on God. The Lord sent prophets to warn, beg, and cajole both nations, relentlessly trying to convince them to turn from their wickedness so they could enjoy a relationship with him. But both Israel and Judah couldn't resist worshiping all the gods of neighboring nations. And since they didn't worship the one true God, they also rejected his rules for living and became an inaccurate reflection of his character. So now, the time had come for drastic action.

———— VIDEO TEACHING NOTES ————

Welcome to session five of *God the Deliverer*. Spend a few minutes sharing any insights or questions about last week's personal study. Then watch the video (see the streaming video access provided on the inside front cover). The answer key is found at the end of the session.

- The divided kingdoms of the north and south, Israel and Judah, had been confronted over and over again by the _____ of God. But they refused to respond. God was finally forced to say, "there is no _____."

- In 722 BC, the northern kingdom of Israel is captured by _____, deported, and assimilated into their pagan culture. They will never really assemble back together again. Today, we call them the "_____ _____ of Israel."

- Like in the northern kingdom, God also raised up _____ in the southern kingdom to give the kings and people his messages. It is time for Judah to hear God's _____ in light of their persistent evil.

- God raises up the _____ to capture Judah, burn down the city of Jerusalem, destroy the beautiful temple that Solomon built, and deport the people to _____. This begins in 605 BC and is complete in 586 BC.

- God tells Jeremiah that before he was even _____,
  he had an idea of what part Jeremiah would play in
  the unfolding of his upper story. Likewise, God already has things in mind for you if you _____
  your life to his upper story.

- Amidst all the tough love and discipline, God tells
  Jeremiah to tell Judah that he is going to bring
  them back _____.

GETTING STARTED

Begin your discussion by reciting the following key verses
and key idea together as a group. Now try to state the key
verses from memory. On your first attempt, use your notes if
you need help. On your second attempt, try to state it completely from memory.

Key Verses: "Because of the LORD's great love we are
not consumed, for his compassions never fail. They
are new every morning; great is your faithfulness"
(Lamentations 3:22–23).

Key Idea: God uses Assyrians in 722 BC to conquer,
deport, and assimilate the kingdom of Israel. They
are lost, never to reassemble as a nation. Overall, the
kingdom of Judah is not markedly better than Israel.
But God has made an unconditional covenant with
David, promising the Messiah would come from David's family in the tribe of Judah. God ultimately

sends the Babylonians in 586 BC to invade Judah and take the majority of the people captive. But he promises that after seventy years, they will return home and continue their part in his grand story.

GROUP DISCUSSION

Take a few minutes with your group members to discuss what you just watched and explore these concepts in Scripture.

1. What part of this week's teaching encouraged or challenged you the most? Why?

2. Why ultimately happened to the kingdom of Israel as a result of their sin?

3. Why was it necessary to also punish the kingdom of Judah for its people's sins?

4. What did God tell Jeremiah to do after the people of Judah were exiled to Babylon?

5. What does Jeremiah reveal will be the "bright spot" in Judah's story?

6. What is your biggest takeaway as you reflect on what you learned this week?

CLOSING PRAYER

End your group time by sharing prayer requests, reviewing how God has answered past prayers, and praying for one

another. Use the space below to record any requests and praises. Also, make sure to pray for people God might add to your group—especially your neighbors.

Name   Request/Praise

_____   _____

_____   _____

_____   _____

_____   _____

_____   _____

_____   _____

_____   _____

FOR NEXT WEEK

Next week, we will look at the story of Daniel and how the Lord showed favor on his people even in the midst of their exile in Babylon. Before your next group meeting, be sure to read through the following personal study, complete the exercises, and memorize the key verses for the session.

VIDEO NOTES ANSWER KEY

messengers, remedy / Assyria, lost tribes / prophets, plan /
Babylonians, Babylon / born, align / home

PERSONAL STUDY

Take some time after your group meeting this week to read through this section and complete the personal study. In total, it should take about one hour to complete. Allow the Scripture to take root in your heart as you review the story of the fall of Israel and Judah.

KNOW THE STORY

It was time for God to act . . . and he did so decisively. According to the Bible, he chose the nation of Assyria to invade the northern kingdom of Israel in 722 BC, defeat it, and deport its citizens back to their own nation. Just like that, Israel ceased to exist. You would think that after witnessing these events, the southern kingdom of Judah would not make the same mistake. But it did . . . and so God raised up the nation of Babylon to invade Judah from 605–586 BC.

> *In the ninth year of Hoshea, the king of Assyria captured Samaria and deported the Israelites to Assyria. He settled them in Halah, in Gozan on the Habor River and in the towns of the Medes.*
>
> *All this took place because the Israelites had sinned against the LORD their God, who had brought them up out of Egypt from under the power of Pharaoh king of Egypt. They worshiped other gods and followed the practices of the nations*

the Lord had driven out before them, as well as the practices that the kings of Israel had introduced. The Israelites secretly did things against the Lord their God that were not right. From watchtower to fortified city they built themselves high places in all their towns. They set up sacred stones and Asherah poles on every high hill and under every spreading tree. At every high place they burned incense, as the nations whom the Lord had driven out before them had done. They did wicked things that aroused the Lord's anger. They worshiped idols, though the Lord had said, "You shall not do this." The Lord warned Israel and Judah through all his prophets and seers: "Turn from your evil ways. Observe my commands and decrees, in accordance with the entire Law that I commanded your ancestors to obey and that I delivered to you through my servants the prophets."

But they would not listen and were as stiff-necked as their ancestors, who did not trust in the Lord their God. They rejected his decrees and the covenant he had made with their ancestors and the statutes he had warned them to keep. They followed worthless idols and themselves became worthless. They imitated the nations around them although the Lord had ordered them, "Do not do as they do."

They forsook all the commands of the Lord their God and made for themselves two idols cast in the shape of calves, and an Asherah pole. They bowed down to all the starry hosts, and they worshiped Baal. They sacrificed their sons and daughters in the fire. They practiced divination and sought omens and sold themselves to do evil in the eyes of the Lord, arousing his anger.

So the Lord was very angry with Israel and removed them from his presence. Only the tribe of Judah was left, and even Judah did not keep the commands of the LORD their God. They followed the practices Israel had introduced. Therefore the LORD rejected all the people of Israel; he afflicted them and gave them into the hands of plunderers, until he thrust them from his presence (2 Kings 17:6–20).

Manasseh was twelve years old when he became king, and he reigned in Jerusalem fifty-five years. His mother's name was Hephzibah. He did evil in the eyes of the Lord, following the detestable practices of the nations the Lord had driven out before the Israelites. He rebuilt the high places his father Hezekiah had destroyed; he also erected altars to Baal and made an Asherah pole, as Ahab king of Israel had done. He bowed down to all the starry hosts and worshiped them. He built altars in the temple of the Lord, of which the Lord had said, "In Jerusalem I will put my Name." In the two courts of the temple of the Lord, he built altars to all the starry hosts. He sacrificed his own son in the fire, practiced divination, sought omens, and consulted mediums and spiritists. He did much evil in the eyes of the Lord, arousing his anger.

He took the carved Asherah pole he had made and put it in the temple, of which the Lord had said to David and to his son Solomon, "In this temple and in Jerusalem, which I have chosen out of all the tribes of Israel, I will put my Name forever. I will not again make the feet of the Israelites wander from the land I gave their ancestors, if only they will be careful to do everything I commanded them and will keep the whole Law that my servant Moses gave them." But the people did not listen. Manasseh led them astray, so that they did more evil than the nations the Lord had destroyed before the Israelites.

The Lord said through his servants the prophets: "Manasseh king of Judah has committed these detestable sins. He has done more evil than the Amorites who preceded him and has led Judah into sin with his idols. Therefore this is what the Lord, the God of Israel, says: I am going to bring such disaster on Jerusalem and Judah that the ears of everyone who hears of it will tingle. I will stretch out over Jerusalem the measuring line used against Samaria and the plumb line used against the house of Ahab. I will wipe out Jerusalem as one wipes a dish, wiping it and turning it upside down. I will forsake the remnant of my inheritance and give them into the hands of enemies. They will be looted and plundered by all their enemies; they have done evil in my eyes and have aroused my anger from the day their ancestors came out of Egypt until this day" (2 Kings 21:1–15).

Jehoiachin was eighteen years old when he became king, and he reigned in Jerusalem three months. His mother's name was Nehushta daughter of Elnathan; she was from Jerusalem. He did evil in the eyes of the LORD, just as his father had done.

At that time the officers of Nebuchadnezzar king of Babylon advanced on Jerusalem and laid siege to it, and Nebuchadnezzar himself came up to the city while his officers were besieging it. Jehoiachin king of Judah, his mother, his attendants, his nobles and his officials all surrendered to him.

In the eighth year of the reign of the king of Babylon, he took Jehoiachin prisoner. As the LORD had declared, Nebuchadnezzar removed the treasures from the temple of the LORD and from the royal palace, and cut up the gold articles that Solomon king of Israel had made for the temple of the

LORD. *He carried all Jerusalem into exile: all the officers and fighting men, and all the skilled workers and artisans—a total of ten thousand. Only the poorest people of the land were left.*

Nebuchadnezzar took Jehoiachin captive to Babylon. He also took from Jerusalem to Babylon the king's mother, his wives, his officials and the prominent people of the land. The king of Babylon also deported to Babylon the entire force of seven thousand fighting men, strong and fit for war, and a thousand skilled workers and artisans. He made Mattaniah, Jehoiachin's uncle, king in his place and changed his name to Zedekiah (2 Kings 24:8–17).

Now Zedekiah rebelled against the king of Babylon. So in the ninth year of Zedekiah's reign, on the tenth day of the tenth month, Nebuchadnezzar king of Babylon marched against Jerusalem with his whole army. He encamped outside the city and built siege works all around it. The city was kept under siege until the eleventh year of King Zedekiah.

By the ninth day of the fourth month the famine in the city had become so severe that there was no food for the people to eat. Then the city wall was broken through, and the whole army fled at night through the gate between the two walls near the king's garden, though the Babylonians were surrounding the city. They fled toward the Arabah, but the Babylonian army pursued the king and overtook him in the plains of Jericho. All his soldiers were separated from him and scattered, and he was captured.

He was taken to the king of Babylon at Riblah, where sentence was pronounced on him. They killed the sons of Zedekiah before his eyes. Then they put out his eyes, bound him with bronze shackles and took him to Babylon.

On the seventh day of the fifth month, in the nineteenth year of Nebuchadnezzar king of Babylon, Nebuzaradan commander of the imperial guard, an official of the king of Babylon, came to Jerusalem. He set fire to the temple of the Lord, *the royal palace and all the houses of Jerusalem. Every important building he burned down. The whole Babylonian army under the commander of the imperial guard broke down the walls around Jerusalem. Nebuzaradan the commander of the guard carried into exile the people who remained in the city, along with the rest of the populace and those who had deserted to the king of Babylon* (2 Kings 24:20–25:11).

This is the word that came to Jeremiah from the Lord: *"This is what the* Lord, *the God of Israel, says: 'Write in a book all the words I have spoken to you. The days are coming,' declares the* Lord, *'when I will bring my people Israel and Judah back from captivity and restore them to the land I gave their ancestors to possess,' says the* Lord.*"* ... *"This is what the* Lord *says:*

"'I will restore the fortunes of Jacob's tents
and have compassion on his dwellings;
the city will be rebuilt on her ruins,
and the palace will stand in its proper place.
From them will come songs of thanksgiving
and the sound of rejoicing.
I will add to their numbers,
and they will not be decreased;
I will bring them honor,
and they will not be disdained.

Their children will be as in days of old,
and their community will be established before me;
I will punish all who oppress them.
Their leader will be one of their own;
their ruler will arise from among them.
I will bring him near and he will come close to me—
for who is he who will devote himself
to be close to me?'
declares the Lord.
"'So you will be my people,
and I will be your God'" (Jeremiah 30:1–3,
18–22).

1. Why did God allow the Assyrians to capture Israel and deport its people?

_____

_____

_____

_____

_____

2. What did God say would happen as a result of Manasseh's actions?

_____

_____

_____

_____

_____

3. What happened to the temple in Jerusalem during the reign of Jehoiachin?

4. What happened when Zedekiah rebelled against the Babylonians during his reign?

5. What promise did God make to his people in captivity through the prophet Jeremiah?

UNDERSTAND THE STORY

In 721 BC, the last king of Israel faced the full wrath of the Assyrian Empire. For years the northern kingdom had paid tribute to Assyria, but in a foolish play for independence, King Hoshea forged a secret alliance with Egypt. The people were soon captured and deported throughout the empire. But the reality is that Israel's downfall had nothing to do with politics gone wrong. Rather, their fall was the result of an unbroken string of idolatrous kings. For the wealthy and powerful among the Israelite elite, a healthy economy had kept them content in their spiritual adultery—until the Assyrian army arrived and it was too late to change.

In contrast to Israel, the southern kingdom of Judah, under the leadership of Hezekiah, chose the Lord as their ally—and God delivered them from the Assyrian threat. But the reprieve was only temporary. Even though Judah had some godly kings (five over a period of 350 years) who attempted to purge the nation of idols, the hearts of the people did not turn fully to the Lord. The situation grew so desperate that eventually the Lord declared that Judah had become as wicked as the people who were in the Promised Land before Israel. In other words, the people God had used to cleanse the land of evil were now in need of cleansing themselves!

This cleansing came in the form of the Babylonian conquest from 605–586 BC. But unlike the northern kingdom of Israel, the Lord determined to preserve the tribe of Judah because of his promise to David that the Messiah would come from his family. After Jerusalem had fallen and the days of judgment were over, God would send them a message of hope and restoration through the prophets Ezekiel and Jeremiah.

Despite God's anger and his judgment, there was still hope for the future. God had not abandoned his promises of a coming Messiah!

1. What do the stories you have read this week reveal about the consequences of failing to heed God's warnings and turn from sin?

2. How do these stories help you understand the consequences of sin?

LIVE THE STORY

It is so easy to fall prey to compromise. Just consider Manasseh of Judah. It is likely he began his reign with every intention of being a godly king like his father. As he was anointed by the high priest, he may have declared his faith in the one true God—and meant it. But then his eye caught the exotic beauty of a golden statue. What harm could come from placing it alongside the altar in God's temple? One could argue that it actually made the temple more beautiful. Before long, one compromise led to another, and the nation fell once again into idolatry. God loves us too much to allow such compromises. He knows that for us to have a relationship with him, it must be pure. He promises us residence in his perfect community forever. All he asks is that we love him—and him *only*—and respond in humble obedience to his guidance.

1. How is God calling you today into a closer relationship with him?

2. What is one action you will take this week to put what you've learned into practice?

TELL THE STORY

One day around a meal or your dinner table, have an intentional conversation about this week's topic with family or friends. During your time together, read Lamentations 3:25–33, and then use the following question for discussion:

> *What are ways we can put our hope in God, seek him, and wait quietly for him?*

Ask God this week to help you fully embrace the story of Israel and Judah's idolatry, the fall of the two kingdoms, and the promise God made that he would restore the Babylonian exiles back to their homeland. Also, spend a few minutes each day committing the key verses to memory: "Because of the LORD's great love we are not consumed, for his compassions never fail. They are new every morning; great is your faithfulness" (Lamentations 3:22–23).

A PROPHET IN EXILE

DANIEL

WELCOME

Consider the high school sophomore who gets up early, goes to campus, stands outside the school with other kids who love God, and prays. They pray for each other, for their leaders, and for their school. Sometimes other kids show up and tease them—even taunt them. But they don't back down. They don't try to explain or defend themselves or act superior. They simply pray—even for the kids who try to ridicule them. Will God honor them for taking such a stand and putting him first? The story we will examine this week provides us with the answer.

VIDEO TEACHING NOTES

Welcome to session six of *God the Deliverer*. Spend a few minutes sharing any insights or questions about last week's personal study. Then watch the video (see the streaming video access provided on the inside front cover). The answer key is found at the end of the session.

- Daniel finds himself away from his home in _____. He is among the first group of people to be exiled—young and elite men who were going to be trained as _____ in the ever expanding pagan nation of Babylon.

- For ten days, Daniel and his friends ate only _____ and drank water. At the end of the ten days, they looked _____ and _____ nourished than any of the young men who ate the rich royal food of the king.

- Nebuchadnezzar makes a decree that anytime the people heard music sounding, they were to stop, bow down, and _____ his statue. Of course, Daniel and his friends _____ to bow down to anybody but God.

- Not only are Daniel and his friends not consumed by the flames, but a _____ appears with them, just walking around. Many scholars believe that this fourth person is none other than the pre-incarnate _____ himself.

- In the lower story, the world may throw us to the _____ or into the _____ _____ for not bowing down to them. But in the upper story, the

King of Kings will stand with us and shut the mouth of the lion for only bowing to him.

- In the upper story, we find ourselves _____ from home. Our home is the new Jerusalem. Therefore, as we walk on foreign soil, we must be resolved not to become _____ to the diet of our culture.

GETTING STARTED

Begin your discussion by reciting the following key verses and key idea together as a group. Now try to state the key verses from memory. On your first attempt, use your notes if you need help. On your second attempt, try to state it completely from memory.

Key Verses: "If we are thrown into the blazing furnace, the God we serve is able to deliver us from it, and he will deliver us from Your Majesty's hand. But even if he does not, we want you to know, Your Majesty, that we will not serve your gods or worship the image of gold you have set up" (Daniel 3:17–18).

Key Idea: The people of the southern kingdom of Judah have been taken into exile, and many now live as residents of Babylon (and later Persia). Among the first exiles taken is a man named Daniel, who along with several other young men, is part of an elite group to be trained as leaders in the empire. Daniel faithfully follows God during his time of exile—in spite of the risks and threats against his life—and never becomes addicted to the "diet" of the culture.

GROUP DISCUSSION

Take a few minutes with your group members to discuss what you just watched and explore these concepts in Scripture.

1. What part of this week's teaching encouraged or challenged you the most? Why?

2. How did Daniel demonstrate his resolve to follow God when it came to eating the Babylonian royal food and drinking the wine?

3. How did Shadrach, Meshach, and Abednego demonstrate their resolve to follow God when it came to the edict to worship the golden statue?

4. After Babylon fell to the Persians, what did Daniel's enemies find to use against him in order to get him thrown into a den of lions?

_____

_____

_____

_____

5. What did Daniel's actions communicate about God to the Babylonians and Persians?

_____

_____

_____

_____

6. What is your biggest takeaway as you reflect on what you learned this week?

_____

_____

_____

_____

_____

CLOSING PRAYER

End your group time by sharing prayer requests, reviewing how God has answered past prayers, and praying for one

another. Use the space below to record any requests and praises. Also, make sure to pray for people God might add to your group—especially your neighbors.

Name   Request/Praise

_____   _____

_____   _____

_____   _____

_____   _____

_____   _____

_____   _____

_____   _____

FOR NEXT WEEK

Next week, we will look at the story of an exile named Esther and see how God orchestrated the events in her life to save his people from extinction. Before your next group meeting, be sure to read through the following personal study, complete the exercises, and memorize the key verses for the session.

VIDEO NOTES ANSWER KEY

Jerusalem, leaders / vegetables, healthier, better / worship, refuse / fourth man, Jesus / lions, fiery furnace / away, addicted

PERSONAL STUDY

Take some time after your group meeting this week to read through this section and complete the personal study. In total, it should take about one hour to complete. Allow the Scripture to take root in your heart as you review the story of Daniel and his friends in exile.

KNOW THE STORY

Daniel and his fellow exiles faced a daunting challenge. How could they lead holy lives in the midst of an unholy culture? Each day, they had to interact with people who embraced false gods, lived sinful lives, and had a radically different mindset. Certainly, taking a stand for God was not always convenient, comfortable, or even safe for them. Yet the example they set reveals how we can likewise live faithfully for God in a culture that is increasingly unfaithful to him.

> *In the third year of the reign of Jehoiakim king of Judah, Nebuchadnezzar king of Babylon came to Jerusalem and besieged it. And the Lord delivered Jehoiakim king of Judah into his hand, along with some of the articles from the temple of God. These he carried off to the temple of his god in Babylonia and put in the treasure house of his god.*
>
> *Then the king ordered Ashpenaz, chief of his court officials, to bring into the king's service some of the Israelites*

*from the royal family and the nobility—young men without
any physical defect, handsome, showing aptitude for every
kind of learning, well informed, quick to understand, and
qualified to serve in the king's palace. He was to teach them the
language and literature of the Babylonians. The king assigned
them a daily amount of food and wine from the king's table.
They were to be trained for three years, and after that they
were to enter the king's service.*

*Among those who were chosen were some from Judah: Daniel, Hananiah, Mishael and Azariah. The chief official gave them
new names: to Daniel, the name Belteshazzar; to Hananiah,
Shadrach; to Mishael, Meshach; and to Azariah, Abednego.*

*But Daniel resolved not to defile himself with the royal
food and wine, and he asked the chief official for permission
not to defile himself this way. Now God had caused the official
to show favor and compassion to Daniel, but the official told
Daniel, "I am afraid of my lord the king, who has assigned
your food and drink. Why should he see you looking worse
than the other young men your age? The king would then have
my head because of you."*

*Daniel then said to the guard whom the chief official had
appointed over Daniel, Hananiah, Mishael and Azariah,
"Please test your servants for ten days: Give us nothing but
vegetables to eat and water to drink. Then compare our appearance with that of the young men who eat the royal food,
and treat your servants in accordance with what you see." So
he agreed to this and tested them for ten days.*

*At the end of the ten days they looked healthier and better
nourished than any of the young men who ate the royal food.
So the guard took away their choice food and the wine they
were to drink and gave them vegetables instead.*

To these four young men God gave knowledge and understanding of all kinds of literature and learning. And Daniel could understand visions and dreams of all kinds.

At the end of the time set by the king to bring them into his service, the chief official presented them to Nebuchadnezzar. The king talked with them, and he found none equal to Daniel, Hananiah, Mishael and Azariah; so they entered the king's service. In every matter of wisdom and understanding about which the king questioned them, he found them ten times better than all the magicians and enchanters in his whole kingdom (Daniel 1:1–20).

At this time some astrologers came forward and denounced the Jews. They said to King Nebuchadnezzar, "May the king live forever! Your Majesty has issued a decree that everyone who hears the sound of the horn, flute, zither, lyre, harp, pipe and all kinds of music must fall down and worship the image of gold, and that whoever does not fall down and worship will be thrown into a blazing furnace. But there are some Jews whom you have set over the affairs of the province of Babylon—Shadrach, Meshach and Abednego—who pay no attention to you, Your Majesty. They neither serve your gods nor worship the image of gold you have set up."

Furious with rage, Nebuchadnezzar summoned Shadrach, Meshach and Abednego. So these men were brought before the king, and Nebuchadnezzar said to them, "Is it true, Shadrach, Meshach and Abednego, that you do not serve my gods or worship the image of gold I have set up? Now when you hear the sound of the horn, flute, zither, lyre, harp, pipe and all kinds of music, if you are ready to fall down and worship the image I made, very good. But if you do not worship *it, you will be thrown immediately into a blazing furnace. Then what god will be able to rescue you from my hand?"*

Shadrach, Meshach and Abednego replied to him, "King Nebuchadnezzar, we do not need to defend ourselves before you in this matter. If we are thrown into the blazing furnace, the God we serve is able to deliver us from it, and he will deliver us from Your Majesty's hand. But even if he does not, we want you to know, Your Majesty, that we will not serve your gods or worship the image of gold you have set up."

Then Nebuchadnezzar was furious with Shadrach, Meshach and Abednego, and his attitude toward them changed. He ordered the furnace heated seven times hotter than usual and commanded some of the strongest soldiers in his army to tie up Shadrach, Meshach and Abednego and throw them into the blazing furnace. So these men, wearing their robes, trousers, turbans and other clothes, were bound and thrown into the blazing furnace. The king's command was so urgent and the furnace so hot that the flames of the fire killed the soldiers who took up Shadrach, Meshach and Abednego, and these three men, firmly tied, fell into the blazing furnace.

Then King Nebuchadnezzar leaped to his feet in amazement and asked his advisers, "Weren't there three men that we tied up and threw into the fire?"

They replied, "Certainly, Your Majesty."

He said, "Look! I see four men walking around in the fire, unbound and unharmed, and the fourth looks like a son of the gods."

Nebuchadnezzar then approached the opening of the blazing furnace and shouted, "Shadrach, Meshach and

Abednego, servants of the Most High God, come out! Come here!"

So Shadrach, Meshach and Abednego came out of the fire, and the satraps, prefects, governors and royal advisers crowded around them. They saw that the fire had not harmed their bodies, nor was a hair of their heads singed; their robes were not scorched, and there was no smell of fire on them (Daniel 3:8–28).

It pleased Darius to appoint 120 satraps to rule throughout the kingdom, with three administrators over them, one of whom was Daniel. The satraps were made accountable to them so that the king might not suffer loss. Now Daniel so distinguished himself among the administrators and the satraps by his exceptional qualities that the king planned to set him over the whole kingdom. At this, the administrators and the satraps tried to find grounds for charges against Daniel in his conduct of government affairs, but they were unable to do so. They could find no corruption in him, because he was trustworthy and neither corrupt nor negligent. Finally these men said, "We will never find any basis for charges against this man Daniel unless it has something to do with the law of his God."

So these administrators and satraps went as a group to the king and said: "May King Darius live forever! The royal administrators, prefects, satraps, advisers and governors have all agreed that the king should issue an edict and enforce the decree that anyone who prays to any god or human being during the next thirty days, except to you, Your Majesty, shall be thrown into the lions' den. Now, Your Majesty, issue the decree and put it in writing so that it cannot be altered—in accordance with the law of the Medes and Persians, which cannot be repealed." So King Darius put the decree in writing.

Now when Daniel learned that the decree had been published, he went home to his upstairs room where the windows opened toward Jerusalem. Three times a day he got down on his knees and prayed, giving thanks to his God, just as he had done before. Then these men went as a group and found Daniel praying and asking God for help. So they went to the king and spoke to him about his royal decree: "Did you not publish a decree that during the next thirty days anyone who prays to any god or human being except to you, Your Majesty, would be thrown into the lions' den?"

The king answered, "The decree stands—in accordance with the law of the Medes and Persians, which cannot be repealed."

Then they said to the king, "Daniel, who is one of the exiles from Judah, pays no attention to you, Your Majesty, or to the decree you put in writing. He still prays three times a day." When the king heard this, he was greatly distressed; he was determined to rescue Daniel and made every effort until sundown to save him.

Then the men went as a group to King Darius and said to him, "Remember, Your Majesty, that according to the law of the Medes and Persians no decree or edict that the king issues can be changed."

So the king gave the order, and they brought Daniel and threw him into the lions' den. The king said to Daniel, "May your God, whom you serve continually, rescue you!"

A stone was brought and placed over the mouth of the den, and the king sealed it with his own signet ring and with the rings of his nobles, so that Daniel's situation might not be changed. Then the king returned to his palace and spent the night without eating and without any entertainment being brought to him. And he could not sleep.

At the first light of dawn, the king got up and hurried to the lions' den. When he came near the den, he called to Daniel in an anguished voice, "Daniel, servant of the living God, has your God, whom you serve continually, been able to rescue you from the lions?"

Daniel answered, "May the king live forever! My God sent his angel, and he shut the mouths of the lions. They have not hurt me, because I was found innocent in his sight. Nor have I ever done any wrong before you, Your Majesty."

The king was overjoyed and gave orders to lift Daniel out of the den. And when Daniel was lifted from the den, no wound was found on him, because he had trusted in his God.

At the king's command, the men who had falsely accused Daniel were brought in and thrown into the lions' den, along with their wives and children. And before they reached the floor of the den, the lions overpowered them and crushed all their bones.

Then King Darius wrote to all the nations and peoples of every language in all the earth:

"May you prosper greatly!

"I issue a decree that in every part of my kingdom people must fear and reverence the God of Daniel.

"For he is the living God
and he endures forever;
his kingdom will not be destroyed,
his dominion will never end.

> *He rescues and he saves;*
> *he performs signs and wonders*
> *in the heavens and on the earth.*
> *He has rescued Daniel*
> *from the power of the lions."*

> *So Daniel prospered during the reign of Darius and the*
> *reign of Cyrus the Persian* (Daniel 6:1–28).

1. What test did Daniel propose to the chief official in regard to the food they would eat?

   _____

   _____

   _____

   _____

2. What were the results of this test?

   _____

   _____

   _____

   _____

3. What caused King Nebuchadnezzar to heat the furnace seven times hotter than usual?

   _____

   _____

   _____

   _____

4. What happened when Shadrach, Meshach, and Abednego were thrown into the furnace?

5. How did God protect Daniel when he was thrown into the lion's den?

UNDERSTAND THE STORY

Daniel and his three friends were probably fifteen or sixteen when they were taken to Babylon. The easiest way for them to make it in this new home would have been to go with the flow and adapt to the Babylonian culture. But that is not what Daniel, Shadrach, Meschach, and Abednego did. Instead, they humbly refused to waver on their convictions.

The men accomplished this first by *resisting bitterness*. Consider how difficult this would have been for them. They had been dragged away to a foreign land—to Babylon, the capital of pagan worship—and disconnected from their families and way of life. They had possibly been made eunuchs and thrown into service for a king they despised and hated. Yet rather than growing bitter about their circumstances, they made themselves useful.

Next, they always *remained respectful*. Rather than simply "taking a stand," they approached their peers and superiors with humility. At the same time, they absolutely refused to compromise on the non-negotiables. If it meant fire or lions, they were willing to sacrifice.

Ultimately, they maintained *hope in God's Word*. Daniel was aware of Jeremiah's prophecy: in seventy years, the exile would end. Daniel's hope was not in his ability to change his circumstances but in the sovereign Lord and his promise. Armed with that hope, Daniel and his friends were able to live lives of significance . . . even in an unholy culture.

1. What do the stories you have read this week reveal about the costs and the benefits of being faithful to God?

_____

_____

_____

_____

_____

2. How will these stories help you to better represent God in your culture?

_____

_____

_____

_____

_____

LIVE THE STORY

As Christians, we live in our own type of Babylon today. For this reason, we should seek to follow Daniel's example by working with *excellence* and putting God *first* in everything we do. Our culture may deem it okay to pad an expense report. But when we turn in an honest report, we put God first by reflecting his values and character. Our culture may say it is okay to gossip. But when we refuse to do so, we put God first by showing respect to others. Our culture may tell us it is important to fit in above all else. But when we refuse to go along when we see an injustice being done, we put God first by treating others as we want to be treated. When Daniel and his friends took a stand, those who did not know their God turned to him. In the same way, when we resist the pull of culture and take a stand for God, it draws others to him.

1. What are some of the "messages" that you have received from society?

2. What is one action you will take this week to put what you've learned into practice?

TELL THE STORY

One day around a meal or your dinner table, have an intentional conversation about this week's topic with family or friends. During your time together, read Daniel 1:11–19, and then use the following question for discussion:

> *What are some of the benefits you have received for taking a stand for God?*

Ask God this week to help you fully embrace the story of Daniel and his friends. Also, spend a few minutes each day committing the key verses to memory: "If we are thrown into the blazing furnace, the God we serve is able to deliver us from it, and he will deliver us from Your Majesty's hand. But even if he does not, we want you to know, Your Majesty, that we will not serve your gods or worship the image of gold you have set up" (Daniel 3:17–18).

THE QUEEN OF BEAUTY AND COURAGE

ESTHER

WELCOME

There are moments in life that feel like a day in Vegas. Sometimes, it seems our fate has been left to the roll of the dice, a shuffle of the cards, or spin of the wheel. The Jewish people in the time of Esther certainly felt this way. At this point, approximately 100 years had passed since the southern kingdom of Judah had been carried into exile. According to God's plan, after 70 years, the Jews had been given an opportunity to head back home. About 50,000 of them did. The rest of them acclimated and became integrated into the Persian culture. They stayed behind—and God remained with them. He is ever present in the events that take place in Esther . . . working behind the scenes to protect and preserve his people.

VIDEO TEACHING NOTES

Welcome to session seven of *God the Deliverer*. Spend a few minutes sharing any insights or questions about last week's personal study. Then watch the video (see the streaming video access provided on the inside front cover). The answer key is found at the end of the session.

- According to God's plan, after _____ years the people of Israel had an opportunity to head back home. Fifty thousand of them did. The rest acclimated and _____ into the Persian society.

- Haman issues an official decree, marked by the king's _____ ring, that gives permission to the people in all 127 provinces of the Persian Empire to kill any Hebrew they come across on one particular _____.

- Through a series of unbelievable events, a young Hebrew girl by the name of _____ becomes the new queen of Persia. She turns out to be the cousin of none other than _____. Talk about luck of the draw!

- Mordecai tells Esther if she doesn't _____ the king for help, some other plan will emerge to provide relief for the people of Israel. We have a choice on whether we will align our lives to God's plan—and receive his _____.

- Esther reveals her identity and requests that the king to save her people from _____. Haman is exposed, and the pole that is meant for Mordecai is now used on him. Mordecai is given Haman's _____ and his entire estate.

- Haman rolled the dice, but God _____ how the dice would fall. The same promise holds true for Christians today.

GETTING STARTED

Begin your discussion by reciting the following key verse and key idea together as a group. Now try to state the key verse from memory. On your first attempt, use your notes if you need help. On your second attempt, try to state it completely from memory.

Key Verse: "For if you remain silent at this time, relief and deliverance for the Jews will arise from another place, but you and your father's family will perish. And who knows but that you have come to your royal position for such a time as this?" (Esther 4:14).

Key Idea: Esther, a young Jewish woman living in Persia, becomes queen around the same time a man named Haman, an Amalekite, is promoted to a position of leadership. Haman has it out for the Jews and convinces the king to sign an edict to exterminate them all on one particular day. However, through

Esther's courage, the tables are turned on Haman and he is executed. The Jews are allowed to arm themselves and thus fend off their extinction.

GROUP DISCUSSION

Take a few minutes with your group members to discuss what you just watched and explore these concepts in Scripture.

1. What part of this week's teaching encouraged or challenged you the most? Why?

2. What did Haman's hatred of Mordecai compel him to do against the Jewish people?

3. How did Esther end up in a place where she could influence the Persian king?

4. What did Mordecai say to Esther to convince her to take a risk for her people?

_____

_____

_____

_____

5. How did God ultimately determine how the "dice" would fall in this story?

_____

_____

_____

_____

6. What is your biggest takeaway as you reflect on what you learned this week?

_____

_____

_____

_____

CLOSING PRAYER

End your group time by sharing prayer requests, reviewing how God has answered past prayers, and praying for one

another. Use the space below to record any requests and praises. Also, make sure to pray for people God might add to your group—especially your neighbors.

Name   Request/Praise

_____   _____

_____   _____

_____   _____

_____   _____

_____   _____

_____   _____

_____   _____

FOR NEXT WEEK

Next week, we will look at the story of the incredible return home from exile for the people of Jerusalem along with the rebuilding of the temple and the city walls. Before your next group meeting, be sure to read through the following personal study, complete the exercises, and memorize the key verses for the session.

VIDEO NOTES ANSWER KEY

seventy, integrated / signet, day / Esther, Mordecai /
approach, blessings / extinction, position / determined

PERSONAL STUDY

Take some time after your group meeting this week to read through this section and complete the personal study. In total, it should take about one hour to complete. Allow the Scripture to take root in your heart and ask God to give you insights into the story of Esther.

KNOW THE STORY

The policy of the Babylonians had been to deport conquered peoples from their homelands in order to suppress any feelings of unity or national identity—and thus quell any rebellions before they began. When the Persians conquered the Babylonians, they took a different approach. Under King Cyrus, the Jewish people were allowed to return to Jerusalem. However, as the story of Esther reveals, many of God's people had adapted to life in the land of their former conquerors . . . "rolling the dice" by putting their fate into the hands of foreign rulers.

> *Later when King Xerxes' fury had subsided, he remembered Vashti and what she had done and what he had decreed about her. Then the king's personal attendants proposed, "Let a search be made for beautiful young virgins for the king. Let the king appoint commissioners in every province of his realm to bring all these beautiful young women into*

the harem at the citadel of Susa. Let them be placed under the care of Hegai, the king's eunuch, who is in charge of the women; and let beauty treatments be given to them. Then let the young woman who pleases the king be queen instead of Vashti." . . .

Mordecai had a cousin named Hadassah, whom he had brought up because she had neither father nor mother. This young woman, who was also known as Esther, had a lovely figure and was beautiful. Mordecai had taken her as his own daughter when her father and mother died.

When the king's order and edict had been proclaimed, many young women were brought to the citadel of Susa and put under the care of Hegai. Esther also was taken to the king's palace and entrusted to Hegai, who had charge of the harem. She pleased him and won his favor. Immediately he provided her with her beauty treatments and special food. He assigned to her seven female attendants selected from the king's palace and moved her and her attendants into the best place in the harem.

Esther had not revealed her nationality and family background, because Mordecai had forbidden her to do so. Every day he walked back and forth near the courtyard of the harem to find out how Esther was and what was happening to her (Esther 2:1–4, 7–11).

After these events, King Xerxes honored Haman son of Hammedatha, the Agagite, elevating him and giving him a seat of honor higher than that of all the other nobles. All the royal officials at the king's gate knelt down and paid honor to Haman, for the king had commanded this concerning him. But Mordecai would not kneel down or pay him honor.

Then the royal officials at the king's gate asked Morde-cai, "Why do you disobey the king's command?" Day after day they spoke to him but he refused to comply. Therefore they told Haman about it to see whether Mordecai's behavior would be tolerated, for he had told them he was a Jew.

When Haman saw that Mordecai would not kneel down or pay him honor, he was enraged. Yet having learned who Mordecai's people were, he scorned the idea of killing only Mordecai. Instead Haman looked for a way to destroy all Mordecai's people, the Jews, throughout the whole king-dom of Xerxes.

In the twelfth year of King Xerxes, in the first month, the month of Nisan, the pur *(that is, the lot) was cast in the pres-ence of Haman to select a day and month. And the lot fell on the twelfth month, the month of Adar.*

Then Haman said to King Xerxes, "There is a certain people dispersed among the peoples in all the provinces of your kingdom who keep themselves separate. Their customs are different from those of all other people, and they do not obey the king's laws; it is not in the king's best interest to tol-erate them. If it pleases the king, let a decree be issued to de-stroy them, and I will give ten thousand talents of silver to the king's administrators for the royal treasury."

So the king took his signet ring from his finger and gave it to Haman son of Hammedatha, the Agagite, the enemy of the Jews. "Keep the money," the king said to Haman, "and do with the people as you please." (Esther 3:1–11).

When Mordecai learned of all that had been done, he tore his clothes, put on sackcloth and ashes, and went out into the city, wailing loudly and bitterly. . . .

So Hathak went out to Mordecai in the open square of the city in front of the king's gate. Mordecai told him everything that had happened to him, including the exact amount of money Haman had promised to pay into the royal treasury for the destruction of the Jews. He also gave him a copy of the text of the edict for their annihilation, which had been published in Susa, to show to Esther and explain it to her, and he told him to instruct her to go into the king's presence to beg for mercy and plead with him for her people.

Hathak went back and reported to Esther what Mordecai had said. Then she instructed him to say to Mordecai, "All the king's officials and the people of the royal provinces know that for any man or woman who approaches the king in the inner court without being summoned the king has but one law: that they be put to death unless the king extends the gold scepter to them and spares their lives. But thirty days have passed since I was called to go to the king."

When Esther's words were reported to Mordecai, he sent back this answer: "Do not think that because you are in the king's house you alone of all the Jews will escape. For if you remain silent at this time, relief and deliverance for the Jews will arise from another place, but you and your father's family will perish. And who knows but that you have come to your royal position for such a time as this?"

Then Esther sent this reply to Mordecai: "Go, gather together all the Jews who are in Susa, and fast for me. Do not eat or drink for three days, night or day. I and my attendants will fast as you do. When this is done, I will go to the king, even though it is against the law. And if I perish, I perish" (Esther 4:1, 6–16).

On the third day Esther put on her royal robes and stood in the inner court of the palace, in front of the king's hall. The king was sitting on his royal throne in the hall, facing the entrance. When he saw Queen Esther standing in the court, he was pleased with her and held out to her the gold scepter that was in his hand. So Esther approached and touched the tip of the scepter. . . .

Then the king asked, "What is it, Queen Esther? What is your request? Even up to half the kingdom, it will be given you."

"If it pleases the king," replied Esther, "let the king, together with Haman, come today to a banquet I have prepared for him." . . .

So the king and Haman went to Queen Esther's banquet, and as they were drinking wine on the second day, the king again asked, "Queen Esther, what is your petition? It will be given you. What is your request? Even up to half the kingdom, it will be granted."

Then Queen Esther answered, "If I have found favor with you, Your Majesty, and if it pleases you, grant me my life—this is my petition. And spare my people—this is my request. For I and my people have been sold to be destroyed, killed and annihilated. If we had merely been sold as male and female slaves, I would have kept quiet, because no such distress would justify disturbing the king."

King Xerxes asked Queen Esther, "Who is he? Where is he—the man who has dared to do such a thing?"

Esther said, "An adversary and enemy! This vile Haman!"

Then Haman was terrified before the king and queen. The king got up in a rage, left his wine and went out into the

palace garden. But Haman, realizing that the king had al-
ready decided his fate, stayed behind to beg Queen Esther
for his life.

Just as the king returned from the palace garden to the
banquet hall, Haman was falling on the couch where Esther
was reclining.

The king exclaimed, "Will he even molest the queen
while she is with me in the house?"

As soon as the word left the king's mouth, they covered
Haman's face. Then Harbona, one of the eunuchs attending
the king, said, "A pole reaching to a height of fifty cubits
stands by Haman's house. He had it set up for Mordecai, who
spoke up to help the king."

The king said, "Impale him on it!" So they impaled Ha-
man on the pole he had set up for Mordecai. Then the king's
fury subsided (Esther 5:1–2; 7:1–10).

The king's edict granted the Jews in every city the right to
assemble and protect themselves; to destroy, kill and annihi-
late the armed men of any nationality or province who might
attack them and their women and children, and to plunder
the property of their enemies. The day appointed for the Jews
to do this in all the provinces of King Xerxes was the thir-
teenth day of the twelfth month, the month of Adar. A copy
of the text of the edict was to be issued as law in every prov-
ince and made known to the people of every nationality so
that the Jews would be ready on that day to avenge themselves
on their enemies.

The couriers, riding the royal horses, went out, spurred
on by the king's command, and the edict was issued in the
citadel of Susa.

When Mordecai left the king's presence, he was wearing royal garments of blue and white, a large crown of gold and a purple robe of fine linen. And the city of Susa held a joyous celebration. For the Jews it was a time of happiness and joy, gladness and honor. In every province and in every city to which the edict of the king came, there was joy and gladness among the Jews, with feasting and celebrating. And many people of other nationalities became Jews because fear of the Jews had seized them (Esther 8:11–17).

1. What elements of Esther's circumstances were beyond her control?

_____

_____

_____

_____

_____

_____

_____

_____

2. How did Mordecai serve the king yet remain faithful to bow only to God?

_____

_____

_____

_____

_____

_____

_____

_____

3. How did Haman convince Xerxes to authorize the annihilation of the Jews?

4. What was Esther's strategy to expose Haman's plot?

5. What was the result of Esther's courage to take a stand
for her people?

UNDERSTAND THE STORY

The story of Esther never explicitly references God, yet we
find evidence of his presence, power, and protection

throughout the account. The theme of God's *sovereignty* particularly shines through in the arrangement of events. First, God orchestrates events so that Vashti, the current queen, is deposed. This allows a Jewish woman named Esther to be raised into her place, where she will be in a position to save her people. The Lord was clearly arranging events for a purpose.

We also see that God uses people to accomplish his purpose. Although the Lord can directly alter history, he often chooses to change the course of history through the actions of his people. We see this in Mordecai, who cared for Esther, raised her, and advised her. When the time was critical, he exhorted her to be courageous. We also see this in Esther, who saw what needed to happen to save her people . . . and then acted bravely to make it happen.

Most importantly, we see that God also *preserves* his people. While he brought punishment and suffering in response to Israel's disobedience, he would not allow *any* power to annihilate them. There were still promises waiting to be fulfilled. In particular, the Lord had promised Abraham that one of his descendants would bring blessing to all nations.

1. What does the story you have read this week reveal about God's sovereignty?

_____

_____

_____

_____

_____

_____

_____

2. How will this story help you to boldly step into the opportunities that God provides?

_____

_____

_____

LIVE THE STORY

What would you do if you were in Esther's place and had to risk everything in order to fulfill God's call on your life? What if your greatest fear, your heaviest burden, had been given to you "for such a time as this" (Esther 4:14)? We may never be in a position where obeying God is a matter of life and death . . . but often God will choose to take us out of our comfort zone to motivate us to take bold risks for him. When this happens, we must follow Esther's example. She immersed herself in prayer and then resolved to do what was right in spite the risks. As a result, an entire race of people were saved. Imagine what could likewise happen in our families, neighborhoods, cities, nations, and world if we all adopted Esther's commitment as our own: "I will go to the king . . . and if I perish, I perish" (verse 16).

1. What are some ways you could model Esther's approach in dealing with problems and setbacks in your life?

_____

_____

_____

2. What is one action you will take this week to put what you've learned into practice?

_____

_____

_____

_____

TELL THE STORY

One day around a meal or your dinner table, have an intentional conversation about this week's topic with family or friends. During your time together, read Esther 4:1–17, and then use the following question for discussion:

What are some examples of how God has placed you in in the right time, place, and position to be involved in his plans?

Ask God this week to help you fully embrace the story of Esther and her decision to take bold risks for God. Also, spend a few minutes each day committing the key verse to memory: "For if you remain silent at this time, relief and deliverance for the Jews will arise from another place, but you and your father's family will perish. And who knows but that you have come to your royal position for such a time as this?" (Esther 4:14).

THE RETURN HOME

EZRA–NEHEMIAH

WELCOME

The Old Testament closes with three building projects. First, the temple is rebuilt under Zerubbabel. Second, the Jerusalem wall is rebuilt under Nehemiah. Third, the people's lives are rebuilt under Ezra. As the priest started to read God's Story to them, they began to weep and mourn. The more he read . . . the louder they wailed. They were heartbroken over their failure to obey. *God's people had finally gotten it!* They had truly returned home to him. Now, the stage was set for the next chapter in their story—and in our stories as well—when God would send his own Son as the promised Messiah.

VIDEO TEACHING NOTES

Welcome to session eight of *God the Deliverer*. Spend a few minutes sharing any insights or questions about last week's personal study. Then watch the video (see the streaming video access provided on the inside front cover). The answer key is found at the end of the session.

- The _____ is rebuilt under the leadership of Zerubbabel. Sacrifices are once again made for sins. The _____ around Jerusalem is rebuilt under Nehemiah's leadership. There is now protection from the people's enemies. But the most important rebuilding project is the rebuilding of the _____ of God's people.

- This has been our _____ as we have gone through the Story—that God would refocus, recenter, and rebuild our lives on his _____ _____.

- The people of Jerusalem began to _____. Why? Because they were hearing God's Word—his love, his desire to be with them, his promise, and his plan to get them back. They were overwhelmed with _____ and joy at the same time.

- The only thing the people did not reinstate is a _____. While there were a few good kings in their history, for the most part, their kings had led them _____.

- The prophet Malachi foretells the next time God speaks—which will be ___ years into the future—it will be through the lips of John the Baptist. He is going to prepare the way for _____ to come.

- It is time for us to meet the one we've been waiting for—God our _____ . Like the Israelites, we need to _____ our hearts to receive this one who is going to give us back our intended life and destiny with God.

GETTING STARTED

Begin your discussion by reciting the following key verse and key idea together as a group. Now try to state the key verse from memory. On your first attempt, use your notes if you need help. On your second attempt, try to state it completely from memory.

Key Verse: "I will send my messenger, who will prepare the way before me. Then suddenly the Lord you are seeking will come to his temple; the messenger of the covenant, whom you desire, will come" (Malachi 3:1).

Key Idea: The children of Israel return from captivity. They rebuild the temple for God's presence to dwell and the wall around Jerusalem to protect themselves from enemies. But the most important project is the rebuilding of their lives with God. Ezra stands before the people and reads God's Story from the beginning. The Israelites weep as they are reminded that God has been writing this epic for ages and has always kept his promises. Malachi, the last person to speak in the Old Testament, foretells that the next prophet who appears will introduce the Messiah—the one who will provide the solution for our restoration with God.

GROUP DISCUSSION

Take a few minutes with your group members to discuss what you just watched and explore these concepts in Scripture.

1. What part of this week's teaching encouraged or challenged you the most? Why?

2. What was the purpose of Ezra reading the Book of the Law to the people?

3. What did the people realize as Ezra began reading God's Story to them?

4. What did the people decide to do after the Law had been read to them?

5. What did Malachi say the next prophet of God would do?

6. What is your biggest takeaway as you reflect on what you learned this week?

CLOSING PRAYER

End your group time by sharing prayer requests, reviewing how God has answered past prayers, and praying for one another. Use the space below to record any requests and praises. Also, make sure to pray for people God might add to your group—especially your neighbors.

Name   Request/Praise

_____   _____

_____   _____

_____   _____

_____   _____

_____   _____

_____   _____

IN THE COMING DAYS

In the days ahead, be sure to read through the following personal study, complete the exercises, and memorize the key verses for the session.

VIDEO NOTES ANSWER KEY

temple, wall, lives / goal, upper story / cry, regret /
king, astray / 400, Christ / Savior, prepare

PERSONAL STUDY

Take some time after your group meeting this week to read through this section and complete the personal study. In total, it should take about one hour to complete. Allow the Scripture to take root in your heart as you review the story of Ezra and Nehemiah's rebuilding projects.

KNOW THE STORY

The people's return to Jerusalem occurred in stages. First, for twenty years under Zerubbabel (c. 538 BC), the temple was rebuilt. Haggai and Zechariah prophesied at that time. Second, for twenty-five years under Nehemiah as governor and Ezra as priest (c. 458–444 BC), the walls were rebuilt. This period unfolded in two stages: (1) Ezra returned for initial work on the walls, and (2) Nehemiah assumed leadership as governor and brought the full support of the Persians to the project. The final Old Testament prophet, Malachi, prophesied during this time.

> In the first year of Cyrus king of Persia, in order to fulfill the word of the LORD spoken by Jeremiah, the LORD moved the heart of Cyrus king of Persia to make a proclamation throughout his realm and also to put it in writing:
> "This is what Cyrus king of Persia says: 'The LORD, the God of heaven, has given me all the kingdoms of the earth

and he has appointed me to build a temple for him at Jeru-salem in Judah. Any of his people among you may go up to Jerusalem in Judah and build the temple of the LORD, the God of Israel, the God who is in Jerusalem, and may their God be with them. . . . ' "

Then the family heads of Judah and Benjamin, and the priests and Levites—everyone whose heart God had moved—prepared to go up and build the house of the Lord in Jerusalem. All their neighbors assisted them with articles of silver and gold, with goods and livestock, and with valu-able gifts, in addition to all the freewill offerings.

Moreover, King Cyrus brought out the articles belong-ing to the temple of the LORD, which Nebuchadnezzar had carried away from Jerusalem and had placed in the temple of his god (Ezra 1:1–3, 5–7).

Then they gave money to the masons and carpenters, and gave food and drink and olive oil to the people of Sidon and Tyre, so that they would bring cedar logs by sea from Leba-non to Joppa, as authorized by Cyrus king of Persia.

In the second month of the second year after their ar-rival at the house of God in Jerusalem, Zerubbabel son of Shealtiel, Joshua son of Jozadak and the rest of the people (the priests and the Levites and all who had returned from the captivity to Jerusalem) began the work. They appointed Levites twenty years old and older to supervise the building of the house of the LORD. Joshua and his sons and brothers and Kadmiel and his sons (descendants of Hodaviah) and the sons of Henadad and their sons and brothers—all Lev-ites—joined together in supervising those working on the house of God.

When the builders laid the foundation of the temple of the LORD, the priests in their vestments and with trumpets, and the Levites (the sons of Asaph) with cymbals, took their places to praise the LORD, as prescribed by David king of Israel. With praise and thanksgiving they sang to the LORD: "He is good; his love toward Israel endures forever."

And all the people gave a great shout of praise to the LORD, because the foundation of the house of the LORD was laid. But many of the older priests and Levites and family heads, who had seen the former temple, wept aloud when they saw the foundation of this temple being laid, while many others shouted for joy. No one could distinguish the sound of the shouts of joy from the sound of weeping, because the people made so much noise (Ezra 3:7–13).

In the month of Nisan in the twentieth year of King Artaxerxes, when wine was brought for him, I took the wine and gave it to the king. I had not been sad in his presence before, so the king asked me, "Why does your face look so sad when you are not ill? This can be nothing but sadness of heart."

I was very much afraid, but I said to the king, "May the king live forever! Why should my face not look sad when the city where my ancestors are buried lies in ruins, and its gates have been destroyed by fire?"

The king said to me, "What is it you want?"

Then I prayed to the God of heaven, and I answered the king, "If it pleases the king and if your servant has found favor in his sight, let him send me to the city in Judah where my ancestors are buried so that I can rebuild it."

Then the king, with the queen sitting beside him, asked me, "How long will your journey take, and when will you get back?" It pleased the king to send me; so I set a time.

I also said to him, "If it pleases the king, may I have letters to the governors of Trans-Euphrates, so that they will provide me safe-conduct until I arrive in Judah? And may I have a letter to Asaph, keeper of the royal park, so he will give me timber to make beams for the gates of the citadel by the temple and for the city wall and for the residence I will occupy?" And because the gracious hand of my God was on me, the king granted my requests. So I went to the governors of Trans-Euphrates and gave them the king's letters. The king had also sent army officers and cavalry with me.

When Sanballat the Horonite and Tobiah the Ammonite official heard about this, they were very much disturbed that someone had come to promote the welfare of the Israelites (Nehemiah 2:1–10).

So we rebuilt the wall till all of it reached half its height, for the people worked with all their heart.

But when Sanballat, Tobiah, the Arabs, the Ammonites and the people of Ashdod heard that the repairs to Jerusalem's walls had gone ahead and that the gaps were being closed, they were very angry. They all plotted together to come and fight against Jerusalem and stir up trouble against it. But we prayed to our God and posted a guard day and night to meet this threat.

Meanwhile, the people in Judah said, "The strength of the laborers is giving out, and there is so much rubble that we cannot rebuild the wall."

Also our enemies said, "Before they know it or see us, we will be right there among them and will kill them and put an end to the work."

Then the Jews who lived near them came and told us ten times over, "Wherever you turn, they will attack us."

Therefore I stationed some of the people behind the lowest points of the wall at the exposed places, posting them by families, with their swords, spears and bows. After I looked things over, I stood up and said to the nobles, the officials and the rest of the people, "Don't be afraid of them. Remember the Lord, who is great and awesome, and fight for your families, your sons and your daughters, your wives and your homes."

When our enemies heard that we were aware of their plot and that God had frustrated it, we all returned to the wall, each to our own work.

From that day on, half of my men did the work, while the other half were equipped with spears, shields, bows and armor. The officers posted themselves behind all the people of Judah who were building the wall. Those who carried materials did their work with one hand and held a weapon in the other, and each of the builders wore his sword at his side as he worked. But the man who sounded the trumpet stayed with me (Nehemiah 4:6–18).

When the seventh month came and the Israelites had settled in their towns, all the people came together as one in the square before the Water Gate. They told Ezra the teacher of the Law to bring out the Book of the Law of Moses, which the LORD *had commanded for Israel.*

So on the first day of the seventh month Ezra the priest brought the Law before the assembly, which was made up of men and women and all who were able to understand. He read it aloud from daybreak till noon as he faced the square before the Water Gate in the presence of the men, women and others who could understand. And all the people listened attentively to the Book of the Law. . . .

They read from the Book of the Law of God, making it clear and giving the meaning so that the people understood what was being read.

Then Nehemiah the governor, Ezra the priest and teacher of the Law, and the Levites who were instructing the people said to them all, "This day is holy to the LORD your God. Do not mourn or weep." For all the people had been weeping as they listened to the words of the Law.

Nehemiah said, "Go and enjoy choice food and sweet drinks, and send some to those who have nothing prepared. This day is holy to our Lord. Do not grieve, for the joy of the LORD is your strength."

The Levites calmed all the people, saying, "Be still, for this is a holy day. Do not grieve."

Then all the people went away to eat and drink, to send portions of food and to celebrate with great joy, because they now understood the words that had been made known to them.

On the second day of the month, the heads of all the families, along with the priests and the Levites, gathered around Ezra the teacher to give attention to the words of the Law. They found written in the Law, which the LORD had commanded through Moses, that the Israelites were to live in temporary shelters during the festival of the seventh month and that they should proclaim this word and spread it throughout their towns and in Jerusalem: "Go out into the hill country and bring back branches from olive and wild olive trees, and from myrtles, palms and shade trees, to make temporary shelters"—as it is written (Nehemiah 7:73–8:3, 8–15).

1. What did Cyrus allow the Jewish exiles to do? What did he provide for them?

2. How was the work on rebuilding the temple in Jerusalem carried out?

3. What bold request did Nehemiah make to the king of Persia?

4. What challenges did Nehemiah face as the people rebuilt the walls of Jerusalem?

_____

_____

_____

_____

_____

5. How did the people acknowledge God as they rebuilt and resettled the land?

_____

_____

_____

_____

_____

UNDERSTAND THE STORY

Whenever you attempt something big for God, you can count on opposition. This is exactly what happened as the exiles began to rebuild the temple in Jerusalem. Dissenters tried everything they could to block their efforts, but God's chosen people maintained their resolve. Day after day, despite interference, they persevered . . . at least for a few years. Then it started to happen. Little by little, they lost their focus. They began to turn less attention to the house of God and more attention to their own personal projects.

Why did this happen? No one knows for sure. Maybe stacking stones was too tiresome. Maybe the criticism was too irksome. Or, more likely, they just started thinking about their own stuff—their businesses, farms, enterprises, houses. One by one, they quit showing up at the worksite. Two years passed. Ten years passed. For sixteen years, the temple project sat untouched! Enough time for all the surrounding nations to look at the temple and think, "Well, they sure don't take their God very seriously."

God's message to Israel—and his message to us—is that he won't be relegated to anyone's closet. He loves us too much to leave us to our own devices. So he pulls us aside for a heart-to-heart chat. He asks us to give careful thought to our ways, wash the mud off the pigpen, and get his work accomplished. Amazingly, this is just what the Jews did. The Lord stirred up the leadership and the people got to work on the house of God. And they finished it.

The lesson stuck. Later, when the Jewish people again faced opposition in rebuilding the wall around Jerusalem, they didn't falter in their resolve. Groups who had been driven out of the land centuries beforehand— Moabites, Ammonites, Ashdodites, and Samaritans—all tried to halt progress and disrupt the work. But under Nehemiah's leadership, the people persisted and finished building the wall rather quickly . . . this time, in a mere fifty-two days!

1. What do the stories you have read this week reveal about the importance of persevering when you are following God's plans?

_____

_____

_____

_____

2. How will these stories help you to better persevere when facing opposition?

_____

_____

_____

_____

LIVE THE STORY

When you look at the story of the rebuilding of the temple . . . you may wonder why God even needed a temple in the first place. Given that he is all-powerful and capable of being everywhere at all times, he could as easily done life with his people without all the trouble of such an elaborate structure. So why bother? The answer is found in the fact the temple served as a *physical reminder* that God wanted to enter into his peoples' lower story. Just consider the location of the temple. It wasn't built atop a mountain, or out in the desert, but was smack-dab in the middle of Jerusalem. Every time anyone walked past it, they were reminded of God's presence. The temple reminded them—and reminds us—that God wants to be with his people.

1. What are some of the ways that God makes his presence known to you today?

_____

_____

_____

_____

2. What is one action you will take this week to put what you've learned into practice?

_____

_____

_____

_____

_____

_____

TELL THE STORY

One day around a meal or your dinner table, have an intentional conversation about this week's topic with family or friends. During your time together, read Haggai 1:5–11, and then use the following question for discussion:

How can we sometimes work for more and more and end up with less and less?

Ask God this week to help you fully embrace the story of Ezra and Nehemiah. Also, spend a few minutes each day committing the key verse to memory: "I will send my messenger, who will prepare the way before me. Then suddenly the Lord you are seeking will come to his temple; the messenger of the covenant, whom you desire, will come" (Malachi 3:1).

LEADER'S GUIDE

Thank you for your willingness to lead your group through this study! What you have chosen to do is valuable and will make a great difference in the lives of others. The rewards of being a leader are different from those participating, and we hope that as you lead you will find your own walk with Jesus deepened by this experience.

God the Deliverer is an eight-session study in *The Story* series built around video content and small-group interaction. As the group leader, just think of yourself as the host of a dinner party. Your job is to take care of your guests by managing all the behind-the-scenes details so that when everyone arrives, they can just enjoy time together.

As the group leader, your role is not to answer all the questions or reteach the content—the video and study guide will do most of that work. Your job is to guide the experience and cultivate your small group into a kind of teaching community. This will make it a place for members to process, question, and reflect—not receive more instruction.

Before your first meeting, make sure the group members have a copy of the study guide. Also make sure they are aware that they have access to the videos at any time through the streaming code provided on the inside front cover. This will keep everyone on the same page and help the process run more smoothly. If some members are unable to purchase the guide, arrange it so they can share the resource with other group members. Giving everyone access to all the material will position this study to be as rewarding an experience as possible. Everyone should feel free to write in his or her study guide and bring it to group every week.

SETTING UP THE GROUP

You will need to determine with your group how long you want to meet each week so that you can plan your time accordingly. Generally, most groups like to meet for either ninety minutes or two hours, so you could use one of the following schedules:

SECTION	90 MINUTES	120 MINUTES
WELCOME (members arrive and get settled)	15 minutes	15 minutes
WATCH (watch the teaching material together and take notes)	15 minutes	15 minutes
DISCUSS (recite the key verse and key idea and discuss study questions you selected)	40 minutes	60 minutes
PRAY (close your time in prayer)	20 minutes	30 minutes

As the group leader, you will want to create an environment that encourages sharing and learning. A church sanctuary or formal classroom may not be as ideal as a living room in this regard, because those locations can feel formal and less intimate. No matter what setting you choose, provide enough comfortable seating for everyone, and, if possible, arrange the seats in a semicircle so everyone can see the video easily. This will make transition between the video and group conversation more efficient and natural.

If you are meeting in person, get to the meeting site early so you can greet participants as they arrive. Simple refreshments create a welcoming atmosphere and can be a wonderful addition to a group study evening. Be sure to take food and pet allergies into account to make your guests as comfortable as possible. You may also want to consider offering childcare to couples with children who want to attend. Finally, be sure your media technology is working properly. Managing these details up front will make the rest of your group experience flow smoothly and provide a welcoming space to engage the content of *God the Deliverer*.

STRUCTURING THE GROUP TIME

Once everyone has arrived, it's time to begin the group. Here are some simple tips to make your group time healthy, enjoyable, and effective.

First, begin the meeting with a short prayer and remind the group members to put their phones on silent. This is a way to make sure you can all be present with one another and with God. Next, watch the video and instruct the participants to follow along in their guides and take notes. After the video teaching, have the group recite the key verse and key idea together before moving on to the discussion questions.

Encourage all the group members to participate in the discussion, but make sure they know they don't have to do so.

As the discussion progresses, you may want to follow up with comments such as, "Tell me more about that," or, "Why did you answer that way?" This will allow the group participants to deepen their reflections and invite meaningful sharing in a nonthreatening way.

Note that you have been given multiple questions to use in each session, and you do not have to use them all or even follow them in order. Feel free to pick and choose questions based on either the needs of your group or how the conversation is flowing. Also, don't be afraid of silence. Offering a question and allowing up to thirty seconds of silence is okay. It allows people space to think about how they want to respond and also gives them time to do so.

As group leader, you are the boundary keeper for your group. Do not let anyone (yourself included) dominate the group time. Keep an eye out for group members who might be tempted to "attack" folks they disagree with or try to "fix" those having struggles. These kinds of behaviors can derail a group's momentum, so they need to be steered in a different direction. Model active listening and encourage everyone in your group to do the same. This will make your group time a safe space and create a positive community.

CONCLUDING THE GROUP TIME

At the conclusion of session one, invite the group members to complete the between-sessions personal studies for that week. Also let them know that if they choose to do so, they can watch the video for the following week by accessing the streaming code found on the inside front cover of their studies. Explain that you will be providing some time before the video teaching the following week for anyone to share any insights. (Do this as part of the opening "Welcome" beginning in session two, right before you watch the video.) Let them know sharing is optional.

Thank you again for taking the time to lead your group and helping them to understand the greater story of the Bible in *God the Deliverer.* You are making a difference in the lives of others and having an impact for the kingdom of God!

God the Deliverer

Our Search for Identity and Our Hope for Renewal

Study Guide
9780310134787

DVD with
Free Streaming Access
9780310134800

This study will introduce you to the lower and upper stories as told in the Old Testament books of 1 Samuel through Malachi to explore how God's plan was at work through the exile and restoration of Israel. As you read these narratives—featuring characters such as Samuel, Saul, David, Jeremiah, Daniel, Esther, Ezra, and Nehemiah—you will see how God has been weaving our lower story into the greater upper story that he has been writing.

Churches can embrace THE STORY for a full ministry year through worship services, small group studies, and family activities.
Learn more about this whole-church experience at TheStory.com.

God the Savior

Our Freedom in Christ and Our Role in the Restoration of All Things

Study Guide
9780310134930

DVD with
Free Streaming Access
9780310134954

This study reveals how God's upper-story plan ultimately came to fulfillment through the birth, ministry, death, and resurrection of Christ. In the New Testament, you will read these stories—featuring characters such as Mary and Joseph, the Twelve Disciples, John the Baptist, Mary Magdalene, the Apostle Paul, and the central figure Jesus Christ—discovering how God has been weaving our lower story into the greater upper story that he has been writing.

HarperChristianResources

If You Want to Grow in Your Faith, You Must Engage God's Word

What you believe in your heart will define who you become. God wants you to become like Jesus—it is the most truthful and powerful way to live—and the journey to becoming like Jesus begins by thinking like Jesus.

Jesus compared the Christian life to a vine. He is the vine; you are the branches. If you remain in the vine of Christ, over time you will produce amazing and scrumptious fruit for all to see and taste. You begin to act like Jesus, and become more like Jesus.

In the **Believe Bible Study Series**, bestselling author and pastor Randy Frazee helps you ask three big questions:

- What do I believe and why does it matter?
- How can I put my faith into action?
- Am I becoming the person God wants me to be?

Each of the three eight-session studies in this series include video teaching from Randy Frazee and a study guide with video study notes, group discussion questions, Scripture reading, and activities for personal growth and reflection.

As you journey through this study series, whether in a group or on your own, one simple truth will become undeniably clear: what you believe drives everything.

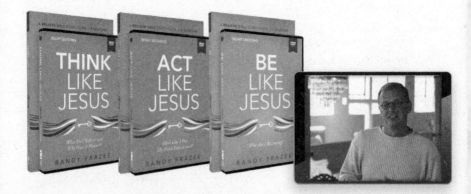

Available now at your favorite bookstore, or streaming video on StudyGateway.com.

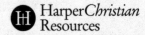